# The
# Girl Without
# a Voice

# CASEY WATSON

*SUNDAY TIMES* BESTSELLING AUTHOR

The
# Girl Without
# a Voice

The true story of a terrified child
whose silence spoke volumes

HARPER
element

This book is a work of non-fiction based on the author's experiences.
In order to protect privacy, names, identifying characteristics,
dialogue and details have been changed or reconstructed.

HarperElement
An Imprint of HarperCollins*Publishers*
77–85 Fulham Palace Road,
Hammersmith, London W6 8JB

www.harpercollins.co.uk

and *HarperElement* are trademarks of
HarperCollins*Publishers* Ltd

First published by HarperElement 2014

1 3 5 7 9 10 8 6 4 2

© Casey Watson 2014

Casey Watson asserts the moral right to
be identified as the author of this work

A catalogue record of this book is
available from the British Library

PB ISBN 978-0-00-751069-6
EB ISBN 978-0-00-751815-9

Printed and bound in the United States of America

Find out more about HarperCollins and the environment at
**www.harpercollins.co.uk/green**

*This book is dedicated to all those who work with children in any capacity. I am filled with admiration for those who strive to make a difference in the lives of those who need someone to listen.*

# Acknowledgements

I would like to thank my wonderful agent, Andrew, and Vicky and her team of super beings at HarperCollins who work tirelessly to ensure my words make it out there. As ever, special thanks to my friend and mentor Lynne, who is there, always, to get me back on track no matter what dramas life bestows.

# Chapter 1

There are jobs and there are jobs, and my perfect kind of job has always been the kind where you wake up Monday morning with no idea what the week might have in store.

Which was exactly the kind of job I *did* have, so it was definitely a blessing that my home life was, in contrast, so predictable.

'Mu-um!' came my daughter's plaintive voice from upstairs. 'I can't find my other black shoe! I have five minutes to get out of the door and I can't find it anywhere! Have you seen it? Someone's *obviously* moved it!'

I shook my head and sighed. That was typical of Riley. She was 18 now and we were so alike, in so many ways. Same black hair, same laugh, same taste in music and fashion. But in one important respect we were different. Where it was my life's mission to try and make the world a tidier place, Riley was the opposite: she was just about the most disorganised person I knew. I knew where her shoe would be. It would, same as ever, be in exactly the same place as it landed when she last flung it off.

I headed upstairs anyway, however, because I had the luxury of an hour till I needed to leave for work, whereas she really did only have five – no, four – minutes. She'd secured a great job after leaving college, and she was really enjoying it. She worked in a travel agents, which she said gave her 'that holiday feeling every day'. But it wasn't a holiday – there was an end time and, more pertinently, a start time. Just as well she had such an understanding boss.

I was halfway up the stairs when she appeared on the landing. 'It's okay,' she said, hopping as she pulled the errant shoe on to her foot. 'Panic over. Someone must have kicked it under my bed.'

'Er, excuse me?' I chided, as she came down to join me. 'Someone? Which someone might that be?'

In answer she planted a quick kiss on my cheek, then she was out of the door to catch her bus with only seconds to spare. I waved her off, thinking wistfully of how it might feel to be 18 again, off to work without a care in the world.

The children in my own world were different. Well, the ones I spent my weekdays with, at any rate. I worked as a behaviour manager in a big inner-city comprehensive school, so the kids that came my way were the opposite of carefree. They came to spend time with me for a variety of different reasons, but what they had in common was that they couldn't cope in a mainstream school setting. My job, as well as providing a safe space in which they could work, was to assess them and decide upon the best course of action, which could involve counselling them, teaching them coping techniques and/or, in some cases, referral to outside agencies that could help them, such as professional counsellors and clinical psychologists. Sometimes it could be as simple as formulating a temporary alternative curriculum, and other times it could end up being protracted and complex – where a child's difficulties were too severe to be dealt with using mainstream school facilities, for example, it might mean a transfer to a live-in establishment that had the staff and facilities appropriate to their needs. And in extreme cases, where the children were deemed to be at risk at home, social services might be brought in and the child placed in care.

Either way, mine was a job that, though often challenging, was never boring, but with the growing numbers of children getting referred to me in the six months since I'd been there, it could also at times be very stressful.

With Riley gone to work, that just left me and my son Kieron at home, with my husband Mike, who was a warehouse manager, long gone too. And home was where I suspected Kieron would stay most of the day. It was the end of September – three weeks into a new academic year – and Kieron was finding life hard to cope with. He was 16 now and had left school back in June without a plan. And with his friends either back in school or college, or even working, he felt a bit rootless – the change in routine had really unsettled him. Kieron has Asperger's, a very mild form of autism, so all change is difficult for him to manage, and the big question – try for college, get a job, do an apprenticeship? – was still to be settled and was weighing heavily on his mind.

And ours too, and would continue to do so till Kieron worked out what he felt was the best path for him; something there would be no point in rushing. No point plunging into something only to find out it was the wrong thing – that would only stress him out more.

So we needed to be patient – though right now I had other things to think about anyway. Having my final cup of coffee, throwing something for dinner into the slow cooker and making sure the house looked the way I wanted it to look when I returned home at the end of the day.

Well, hopefully, anyway. I gave my work shoes a quick polish before slipping them on my feet and grimacing at my reflection in the hall mirror. That was the one major downside of doing what I did – that I had to get so trussed up to do it. Smart black skirt and jacket, black tights, shiny shoes. And a crisp stripy blouse – it was all so not me! I've always been much more of a jogging bottoms and T-shirt type, more a 'bundle my unruly hair any-which-way into a ponytail' sort of woman than one who enjoys spending hours in front of a mirror blow-drying it and having to wear make-up all day.

But there was no choice, not if I wanted to be seen as a professional. Part of my job involved meetings with fellow professionals – head teachers, social workers, educational welfare staff, educational psychologists – so I had learned quickly what the sartorial rules were. I needed to dress to impress if I was going to by taken seriously – an uncomfortable sacrifice for someone like me. I'd rather spend time with a hundred unruly teenagers than be sat around a conference table with adults of that calibre – intimidating was what it was, even if necessary.

As ever, however, all thoughts of anything other than the job in hand left my mind as soon as I walked through the school gates, and I was greeted by the usual cacophony of shrieks and yells that were synonymous with every Monday morning.

'Morning, Miss – did you have a nice weekend?'

'Miss! Brandon Smith's been telling lies about me!'

'Mrs Watson, can I come to you instead of doing PE today?'

Smiling at the little crowd that threatened to engulf me, I pointed at the oversized hall clock. 'We'll have plenty of time to catch up later,' I reassured the group around me. 'And yes, I did have a nice weekend, thank you, but right now it's time you all got off to registration.' I grinned at them. 'And guess what I need?'

'Coffee!' came the chorus, as the kids began dispersing. 'Coffee, Miss, you're off to get your coffee!'

They weren't wrong. My love of coffee was almost as well known about me as my love of creating order out of chaos. Not that the staffroom was chaos, exactly, but neither was it a shrine to housewifery. I knew I was regularly the subject of whispers and odd looks as I stood by the drinks-making area in the corner, furiously wiping spills and polishing teaspoons. I'd often wait behind, too, after the bell had gone for classes, plumping cushions and straightening papers and journals. No one ever mentioned it – well, not to me, not yet, at any rate, but I was pretty certain they knew it was me.

There was the usual air of sudden evacuation in the room as I entered, as the assembled teachers – often 25 or so at this time of day – headed to their classes to deal with registration. I, on the other hand, still had half an hour to kill, as the students currently with me would not come to my classroom till after that was over, at around 9.30. I made my coffee, trying to resist the urge to do the washing-up as well. Which was ridiculous; there was a lady whose job it was to come in and do that during lesson time, but it was a challenge for me not to beat her to it.

Still, I resisted. I had plenty to be doing anyway. There were the lesson plans for each child in my unit to be final-ised – currently five – plus some writing-up of stuff from the previous day. I did a daily 'life space' interview with every child who was with me. It was one of the new buzzwords, and what it actually meant was starting a conversation off with each child and then just listening. Well, not just listening – 'active' listening, which was all about helping the child to open up, using emotive prompts such as 'That must have been upsetting for you' and 'What happened then?'

And going by my experience with some of the kids I'd had pass through my hands so far, the answer to that could be *anything*. Straighteners or not, it could make anyone's hair curl.

My office was situated on the ground floor of one of the two school buildings, the one that also housed most of the other main offices and the art, sport and drama depart-ments. The second building, which was connected to the first via a long corridor and the main dining hall, was where the majority of the normal classrooms were.

Though 'office' was perhaps too fine a word for my new room. In truth, it was an old, long disused, tiny classroom that had once been a learning support room. Back in the day, it had housed 15 or so pupils, and had contained nothing but a few tables and chairs and an elderly blackboard when I first viewed it. The head, Mr Moore, had been surprised that I'd chosen it over the alternatives he'd shown me. There'd also been a large airy office that had once housed Mr Brabbiner, the deputy head, or a laboratory-style classroom with huge built-in desks, an interactive whiteboard and a separate office area.

But no. This was the one I'd wanted. Though it had been both filthy and gloomy when I saw it, what I also saw was loads of potential. And the main reason for that had been the pair of 'French doors'. Actually a fire exit, they opened out onto a lovely sheltered grassy area, and, best of all, there was no rule that said I had to keep them closed. In short, it had a garden, and I was immediately won over, and asked if I could come in for two weeks before I actually started so I could get the place properly cleaned and organised.

I looked at it now, and smiled. It really was my home from home. I had set aside an area for myself, using a couple of tables to create an 'L' shape, and behind that I kept a kettle and cups, everything I needed to make drinks with, plus a toaster and the thing I had quickly become known for – having always, but *always*, a supply of biscuits.

I'd had the caretaker paint the whole room a sunny shade of yellow (which was about as outrageous a hue as the council allowed), and made brightly coloured frames which I hung on all the walls to house the works of art I didn't doubt I'd soon be getting. With the garden in mind (I had ambitious designs on that too) I also made an area for plants and seed potting. That initiative, too, got me a few choice looks from colleagues, as I lugged bags of compost down the corridors.

Finally, I installed a radio, and a chill-out area come mini-library, complete with a low table and some luridly patterned bean bags.

Only then did I arrange study tables and chairs in the centre, in what space was left available for the purpose. This was a classroom, no doubt about it, but it was so much more than that. It was to be a place where troubled kids could properly chill out and feel relaxed, whatever the reason for them being in my 'office'. And that mattered. It was so much easier to talk to a relaxed child than a stressed one that, though I did wince when I saw how much I'd spent from my meagre budget, I didn't feel guilty. I felt justified. I'd made it as it should be.

My gang of 'regulars' arrived with the usual kerfuffle. Kids came and went, obviously – some would be with me for just a lesson or two – but a few were with me full time during any given week. I had five of those with me currently, and they couldn't have been more different. I had three year 7s – new to the school, still finding their way for various reasons, and two year 8s who'd both come to me last term.

First in, and most challenging, was Henry. Aged 13, he was in danger of permanent exclusion due to his disruptive and frequently violent nature. He'd already been excluded from lessons by almost all of his teachers, and coming to my 'Unit' (not my name of choice – I hated labels, but it had well and truly stuck now) was a last-ditch attempt to get him to settle down sufficiently that he could stay in mainstream education.

This morning, happily, he seemed to be in high spirits. 'All right, Miss?' he said as he bounced into the room and slung his tatty backpack down on the nearest table.

'I'm fine, Henry,' I told him. 'And you're sounding chirpy. Have a good weekend?'

'Miss, it was *epic*.'

Henry's problem with the world seemed to be rooted in a lack of empathy. He was the youngest of five boys, living with a mum on benefits – there was no dad on the scene – and it seemed he struggled with his place in the home hierarchy. He'd only ever had hand-me-downs (clothes and toys) for obvious reasons, which didn't automatically mean he'd be emotionally scarred – far from it; lots of kids had next to nothing and were fine. But Henry wasn't. His main problem seemed to be that he was treated as the runt of the family, getting picked on mercilessly by his older brothers. He would then, understandably, come into school full of anger, and would then transfer that to children younger or smaller than him. He was also unkempt and dirty, which was another of his issues – one of the things I'd already been able to establish was that one particular teacher had tended to pick on him too – showing him up in front of the other kids. In fact the first indication I'd had that I could perhaps make some progress with Henry was when he confided that this teacher had humiliated him in front of everyone. 'I always know when you've arrived in class, Henry,' he told him, 'because you're quickly followed by a bad smell.'

But he seemed in good spirits this morning, and full of what had obviously been a good weekend, and I didn't doubt he'd have been about to tell me why it had been so 'epic', only at that point he was joined by another of my current trio of boys, who, there being some important footballing victory to be discussed, immediately commanded his attention. Gavin, who was 11 and had just joined the school, had ADHD ; he was on Ritalin and had been sent to me for a 'calming' period of two months, to try and help improve his behaviour and concentration.

Third to arrive was Ben, who was new to both school and area. He'd been excluded from his primary before the end of the last school year and had not been in education for six months. Ben lived with his dad, his mum having died shortly after giving birth to him, and, for a million reasons, he was angry all the time. My job with Ben, in the short term, was simply to assess him, so that some sort of strategy could be developed to help soothe his troubled soul.

And Ben wasn't the only child who was bereaved. Shona, too – a sweet 12-year-old – had lost both her parents. Leaving Shona, an only child, with an uncle, aunt and cousins, they'd gone on a brief second honeymoon and been killed in a car crash when travelling home from the airport.

Shona, who was understandably finding it difficult to cope, had been with me since not long after I'd taken up my post. My heart went out to her, but there at least seemed to be a little progress. Since the arrival of Molly – another newbie with slight learning difficulties – she seemed to have found a new focus and sense of purpose. Helping Molly, who had been a target for bullies since starting school three weeks back, seemed to bring some light to Shona's dark, unhappy days.

They came in side by side, as they invariably did, and both smiled at me as they parked their coats and bags. Though, on this occasion, there was a third person coming through the door behind them – Donald Brabbiner, the deputy head.

'You have a moment, Mrs Watson?' he asked me, indicating that I should step out into the corridor.

'Of course,' I said, turning automatically to the children. 'Get yourselves organised,' I told them. 'We're going to be continuing with what we were doing Friday. So start getting your equipment out. *Quietly*.'

I followed Don out, smiling to myself as the three boys immediately took on that slightly anxious 'Oh God, what am I in trouble for?' expression. Don was a great deputy head and a real presence around the school. And, having been in post for several years now, also something of a legend.

We stepped outside and I pulled the door towards me. 'Problem?'

'No, no,' he reassured me, smiling. 'Nothing to worry about. I was just wondering how many you had in today that's all. Is it just those five?'

I nodded. 'Though I think I've got a couple more coming after lunch. Why?'

'Because we've got a new girl – a 13-year-old. Name of Imogen. She's new to the area as well as the school, and it looks like she might need to come straight to you. Arriving some time in the next hour – I think her grandparents are bringing her. I told them to try to arrive before first break.'

'You know anything else yet?'

'Not a great deal,' Donald answered. 'It's all a little bit last minute, this, to be honest.'

'That's fine,' I said. 'I dare say we'll find out soon enough, won't we? I'll come round to your office when they get here then, shall I? And we can all sit down and have a little chat.'

'Ah,' Donald said, shaking his head. 'A chat is precisely what we *won't* be having with her – in fact, that's the reason she needs to go into your Unit.'

'I don't get you,' I said, grinning. 'What is she – feral?'

Don shook his head. 'Though it is a bit bizarre,' he explained. 'First time I've come across something like this, to be honest.'

'As in?' I prompted.

'As in she doesn't speak.'

'What, not at all?' I asked, confused. 'Is she disabled?'

'Apparently not. Just doesn't speak in certain situations – I understand it's called selective mutism. Except that at the moment it appears the "selective" bit is absent. Hasn't spoken for weeks now, apparently. Not at all.'

Well, well. That was something I'd never come across before either. My line of work frequently involved dealing with the opposite problem, and though I also dealt with shy kids who needed coaxing from their shells, a child who didn't speak at all was something else again.

I went back into my 'Unit' and considered my current charges, who, according to type, were variously talking in whispers or babbling away at each other thirteen to the dozen. Till they saw me and fell into a predictable silence, that was – a state of affairs anyone working in a school should work hard to be able to bring about with ease.

What a thing, I decided, to have a child in your care in whom you want to provoke the exact opposite. Well, we'd see. It might not be Riley's 'every day's a holiday', this job of mine, but there was no doubt that it was always an adventure.

# Chapter 2

Getting my job at the comp was something of a dream come true for me, and I still pinched myself sometimes that I had. Yes, I'd worked with young people before, but never in a school setting, so to be entrusted with a job looking after the school's most challenging children was something I felt very proud of.

My background had previously been in social services. I'd had a similar role, in that I was helping the disadvantaged and troubled, but it had involved working with adults – ones with learning disabilities. So though I'd done teacher training and managerial courses as part of my post with social services, my only prior experience of supporting and helping troubled kids had been when I'd been a volunteer youth worker.

I don't know what clinched it on the day. There were four of us interviewed, and I never in a million years thought I'd get it, because the other candidates had way more professional qualifications. But I did. 'The head phoned me personally,' I told Mike, when I called him to tell him the good news. 'Said it was my obvious understanding of how the school were trying to be more proactive about the emotional well-being of their pupils that had swung it,' I explained. 'That and my enthusiasm, which had apparently *really* impressed him. And he said they'd pay for any courses I needed to go on.'

'And?' Mike had asked.

'And what?' I'd answered.

'And how many unmarked £50 notes did you have to slip him?'

No danger of anyone getting a big head in our house.

I had never worried that I might become bored or disillusioned once the reality of working in a large city comprehensive kicked in, but neither had I reckoned on how much the job would consume me. It was just so engrossing – sometimes stressful, sometimes fascinating, but always so interesting – that on weekdays, at any rate, I ate, slept and breathed it.

And it looked like this week would be no exception. A new child always brought a little thrill of excitement, as each one was a different leap into the unknown. And this one sounded particularly intriguing. I made a mental note to see if I could find out anything about selective mutism on my computer once the children were settled with their work.

'Right,' I told them. 'Let's get this project up in the air, shall we?'

Henry, predictably, groaned at my pun. We had been doing a project on the history of aviation for the past two weeks, and had been devoting the first two hours of each day to developing it. My little group were lucky. Only the school's IT department enjoyed the luxury of computers, and the only internet connections were on the ones in the school offices. But since my classroom was also my office, that meant I had one of those precious few, so could allow access to the children in my care for their research. And the boys had researched well. And, now, armed with all the information they needed, they had been making a magnificent model of the Wright Brothers' first plane together with an accompanying narrative.

The girls, meanwhile, had been busy writing a first-person account of Amelia Earhart's solo flight across the Atlantic. The whole group had also been working on a large timeline poster, complete with carefully cut-out pictures and artwork. They'd all worked hard, and I was proud of them, and would feel even prouder when they presented their work during school assembly the following week.

They worked quietly and productively for a good 20 minutes, when Henry's hand suddenly shot up. 'Miss,' he said, waving it impatiently, as ever. 'We've been wondering – who's going to do all the talking when we do our presentation?'

Which, when decoded, meant 'would it be him?' He was very aware of his status as the oldest in the group, as he would be, given his background.

I walked across and sat down at the boys' table. I mixed them up sometimes but most of the time the three boys sat at one and the girls at another. It was good to make them work together, obviously, but only up to a point. Most of the time, my number one priority was to have these kids relaxed and receptive – and that meant making them feel as comfortable as possible.

'Well, that's for you to decide. All five of you. You'll have to get together and have a board meeting about it.'

Ben giggled and nudged Henry. 'Bored meeting, more like. It *will* be a bored meeting if Molly and Shona have to speak!'

I glanced across at the girls, but they hadn't even heard. They were, as ever, bent over their work, heads close, engrossed. 'Don't be silly, Ben,' I said. 'You know I don't mean that sort of bored. No, you'll have to have a meeting and discuss it. Though I think it would be nice if you all had something to say, don't you? You've all worked so hard on this that you all deserve the spotlight, don't you think? Anyway, right now, I need you to all get on, so we can get it finished. And quietly, please, because I need to go and make a phone call.'

I left the kids to it and went across to my desk in the corner, where I buzzed the Learning Support department in search of my sometime assistant, Kelly.

Kelly was a 23-year-old teaching assistant who had a wonderful rapport with the more challenging pupils, which meant she was very sought after within the school.

She answered the phone herself, and pre-empted my question. 'Hi,' she said. 'I know what you're going to ask and I'll be down in ten minutes. I saw Mr Brabbiner earlier and he put me in the picture.'

'Brilliant,' I said. 'They're working on their project right now, too. So you shouldn't have any problems.'

Kelly laughed. She knew as well as I did that things could change in a split second. One minute everything could be hunky dory – as it was now – and the next all hell could break loose. Still, that was what I liked about her, and what set her apart from some of the other TAs – she seemed to thrive on the unknown element of it all, just as I did, and I'd yet to see her faced with anything she couldn't handle. She was an expert at thinking on her feet.

I went to sit with the girls for a bit once I'd put down the phone, and had what had become a predictable response from Molly once I'd told them I'd be gone for a bit and that Miss Vickers would be looking after them. She glanced at the boys nervously. 'You won't be gone long, will you, Miss? We don't like it when you leave us, do we, Shona?'

Shona put a protective arm around her friend. 'Miss Vickers is all right, Molly,' she reassured her. 'She won't stand for any nonsense, will she, Miss?'

'No, she won't,' I agreed, smiling at her grown-up turn of phrase. 'And there will be no nonsense. Will there, boys?' I added, raising my voice so they could hear me. 'Or it'll be maths practice all afternoon.'

'Where you going anyway, Miss?' Shona wanted to know.

'To a meeting,' I said. 'Not a board meeting but a meeting about a new girl who might be joining us. Her name's Imogen and we need to see if she's going to be right for us. I'll be able to tell you more once I've been and met her.'

Both Shona and Molly exchanged looks (girls and threes didn't readily blend well – it took time and management), but it was Gavin who spoke up. 'Another *girl?*' he moaned.

'We don't want to be invaded by no more girls, Miss. Is she a retard?'

'Gavin!' I admonished. 'What have I told you about name-calling? Have you remembered nothing of the exercise we did the other week?'

His brow furrowed a little as he tried to recall what I meant. We'd done an exercise I tried to fit into the schedule periodically – splitting the kids into two groups and having each one draw a picture of a gingerbread man. This wasn't in any sense an art exercise, though. I'd then get one set to annotate theirs with any horrible names they had ever called anyone. And with no holds barred – swear words were acceptable on this occasion, if that had been the way the thing had been said. The other group had to do likewise, only this time they had to record any names they recalled having *been* called, by either adults or other children. I would then swap the drawings over and ask each group to write down how they would feel or how they felt when they had been called any name from the list, and then compile a separate list of reasons why they thought people might call others by these names.

It was all about developing their emotional literacy; a key part of what my role was in the Unit. And, judging by Gavin's comment, perhaps I needed to revisit it some time soon.

'Well?' I said to him.

'Sorry, Miss,' he mumbled. 'I didn't mean nothing. Just wanted to know what she would be, like, doing here.'

'Then you need to think harder about how you're going to say something *before* you say it,' I told him. 'Because if I hear any more talk like that you *will* be doing maths practice all afternoon, is that clear?'

I wasn't too worried about Gavin, however. He'd had his morning dose of Ritalin and it would be another couple of hours before his ADHD became blindingly obvious again. Then it would be another hour before he was given his meds by the school nurse – an hour when it would be hard for me to leave the classroom. Even Henry, who at 13 was two years Gavin's senior, didn't like what he called 'the mad hour'.

I smiled at my trio of lads; they'd actually come on really well in terms of behaviour, even though to the casual observer their improvements might seem tiny. But they were still angry little lads, all three of them like tightly coiled springs, and much as we had calm days, we also had the other kind – days when I seemed to be permanently braced and waiting for the next unexpected explosion. It would be a volatile place for this new girl to try and fit in to, there was no doubt about that.

Kelly arrived bang on cue, clutching two mugs of coffee, one of which I saw was in my superhero mug – it had Batman on one side and Spiderman on the other, and had been a 'new job' surprise gift from Kieron. And to date, no one had accidentally walked off with it either; a minor miracle in a school staffroom, apparently. She held it out to me.

'Here,' she said. 'Thought I'd make you one while I was at it.' Then she smiled at the children. 'You all look like very busy bees. Everything okay?'

They nodded dutifully. 'Thanks, love,' I said to her. 'That's thoughtful.' I had my little 'coffee corner' but didn't always get round to filling the kettle, so the mug of my preferred stimulant was very welcome. 'I imagine I'll only be an hour or so, maybe less. But you shouldn't encounter any problems.'

Kelly grinned, pulling out her walkie-talkie from her pocket. 'Don't worry – I'm packing my secret weapon. We'll be fine.'

Most of the teachers, and some of the support staff, like Kelly, had access to these contraptions so they could call for duty staff to come and help out in an emergency. This might involve something as simple as a child being asked to leave the class due to disruptive behaviour or, in more extreme cases, an extra pair of hands to help break up a physical fight. They were called Computerised Communications Units (CCUs) but I was the resident oddball because I never used mine. I hated new techno gadgets so relied on my new mobile phone – another piece of kit I had yet to fully master.

I grabbed it now and popped it in my handbag. Unlike the majority of the staff, I always kept the latter with me too, partly because with such a small group situation it was easy enough to keep an eye on, and partly because it was akin to a Mary Poppins handbag – something that had developed since Kieron was little. Him being the way he was, it had often been a lifesaver; if he got dirty or cut himself he'd be more upset that he looked dishevelled than if he hurt himself.

It was a lifesaver with the kids in school too. I always had tissues, packs of plasters, biscuits, sweets and even make-up, which always proved popular when girls got upset – a bit of lip gloss and a spot of blusher always cheered them up.

'Right,' I said, picking up the bag. 'I'm off. And remember, everyone, I can whip up a maths lesson in seconds if need be, so, best behaviour while I'm gone.'

I walked quickly through the corridors before the bell went that would signal break time, along with the inevitable stampede of children rushing off to the tuck shop and the playground. It went just as I arrived outside Donald's office's closed door.

I opened it to find Donald and the family all assembled, the latter with their backs to me, facing his desk.

'Ah, Casey,' said Donald, rising. 'Come in.' He pointed to the remaining seat, which was positioned to the side of the desk. 'This is Mrs Watson,' he said to the assembled trio as I slipped past them and sat down on it. 'She's the one I told you about on the phone, and who'll hopefully be looking after young Imogen here.'

I smiled and, now that I could see them, took in the row of people. The two grandparents – who were white-haired and both looked to be in their mid-seventies – and Imogen herself, a girl you really couldn't miss; not with that veil of ginger hair – well, more strawberry blonde, actually; that's what I'd have called it. But I knew kids. It was red. They'd call it ginger.

'Good morning,' I said, extending a hand. 'Mr and Mrs …'

'Hinchcliffe,' the woman provided. 'I'm Veronica,' she added, accepting it. Her hand, like the rest of her, was small

22

and frail-looking. 'And this is Mick. We're Imogen's grand-parents,' she added. 'She lives with us.'

Her voice was clipped and I could see by the way she was holding herself that she was nervous, though her husband – a huge, fit-looking man who had only acknowledged my arrival with a nod – seemed more interested in watching the swarm of excitable children who were now rushing, whooping and shouting, past Donald's office window. I had the feeling it had been a while since he'd been exposed to so many youngsters all at once.

I turned to Imogen herself, but she didn't seem to want to make eye contact. She just stared out of the same window, a blank expression on her face.

'Imogen,' prompted her grandmother, obviously seeing the direction of my gaze. 'Did you hear Mr Brabbiner? This is Mrs Watson, your new teacher.'

Now Imogen did turn, blinking once as our eyes met, then lowering her head.

'She won't talk,' Mrs Hinchcliffe said, looking pained. 'Not here. Not anywhere. Can't shut her up at home, of course.'

'Oh, I said, glancing at Don. 'So she is still speaking sometimes, then?'

Mrs Hinchcliffe nodded. 'The doctor says it's something called selective mutism. That she's just choosing *not* to talk. Though for the life of us we can't work out why.'

I nodded. 'Don't worry too much,' I said. 'I'm sure Imogen will be fine with us, won't you?' I turned to Imogen as I said this but she didn't raise her head. 'But can I ask you,' I went on, conscious that I wasn't completely comfortable discussing Imogen while she was in the room with us, but that, as she didn't seem to want to contribute, there was really little choice, 'why this school at this time? Where was she previously?'

Now the grandfather spoke. 'We took her out of her other high school at the end of the summer term. Had to. She'd been fine before all this started – you know, moving in with us and everything. But when it did start happening, they were useless. All the other kids started picking on her and the teachers were no help at all. Just thought she was being awkward. It's not right ...'

Donald slid a file across the desk to me. 'These are all Imogen's notes from her previous school, Mrs Watson. I've obviously explained to Mr and Mrs Hinchcliffe that we can take Imogen, no problem, though, in terms of her mutism, I'm not actually sure how much help we can be. Though she does apparently have a therapist working with her at home now, doesn't she, Mrs Hinchcliffe? So ...'

'A child psychologist, is what it is,' Mr Hinchcliffe interrupted. 'Load of mumbo jumbo, if you ask me.' He scowled, though more in frustration, I thought, than in irritation. 'The girl needs to sort herself out. Choosing when and where to speak ...'

Imogen didn't react in any way but I could see Don was looking uncomfortable. Perhaps more had been said before I'd entered. There was clearly some tension in the room. 'Well,' I said brightly, deciding to take charge of the situation, 'there's no need for us to go into all the ins and outs right now, and no point in Imogen being out of school any longer than she has to. If she has some uniform,' I said, looking at her, but still seeing the top of her head mostly, 'she could start tomorrow, if you like.'

I looked at Don, who signalled he was fine with that happening. 'Or,' I added, as it occurred to me, 'if she doesn't, I can perhaps help. We have a good stock of school logo sweatshirts at the moment, so, if you'd like me to find her one, it's just a case of you kitting her out in a black skirt or trousers and a white shirt.'

Don's expression changed now, at my off-message largesse. I was actually meant to try and sell the stock of surplus uniform, but I got the impression money was tight and I had a good stock of sweatshirts in my room. I was the lost property queen of the school, after all.

I stood up, picked up the file and extended my hand to the couple once again. 'So if that's it for now,' I said, 'I really need to get back to my class.'

Everyone else stood up too. 'No, no, that's fine,' agreed Don. 'We'll see you tomorrow then, Imogen.'

'Indeed you will,' said Mrs Hinchcliffe. 'Come on sweetheart,' she said, nudging her granddaughter to stand up as well. 'Come on, let's get you home for some lunch, shall we?'

Imogen duly stood and only now could I see just how small she seemed to be for 13: small and slight and dressed in clothes that looked old and, more importantly, old fashioned – nothing like the clothes worn by most of her peer group. She was a pretty girl, with deep blue eyes, pale skin and a liberal sprinkling of freckles. I felt sorry for her. I somehow knew, even without checking, that this was an only child. No older siblings to help with fashion tips and general 'fitting in' type guidance. A lonely kid, I guessed, who found it hard to make friends. A ready target for bullies. Definitely that.

It felt all wrong to have been talking over her, even if there wasn't really an option, since they'd brought her. Which was understandable – they wanted her to see the school for herself, of course they did. But it didn't really make for a productive meeting. There were so many questions I'd have liked to ask, all of them personal, but that would have to wait till I had a chance to speak to Imogen's grandparents alone. For now, I had only my gut instinct to rely on, and my gut instinct, as I watched them go, was that there was a lot going on here. That the grandfather's insistence that they had no idea why their granddaughter had developed selective mutism was – without a doubt – not quite true.

# Chapter 3

After a quick lunch and catch-up with Kelly in the staff-room, I made it back to my classroom only seconds before the bell went, with the usual accompanying surge of small purposeful bodies, almost all of whom were ignoring the equally familiar teachers' shouts of 'Walk, please!', 'Don't run!' and 'Keep *left*!'

'Miss, what we doing this afternoon?' asked Shona, as I flicked on my kettle. 'Not *really* maths, is it? Can't me and Molly do some art?'

I spooned a large teaspoon of coffee into my mug. 'Not maths, love, don't worry. And we're going to do something that *is* a bit like art, actually. It's –'

But I was prevented from replying by the arrival of Gavin, bursting through the door like a small-boy-shaped battering ram, his ADHD medication clearly not yet having taken full effect. 'Whoosh whoosh!' he yelled, obviously pretending to be an aeroplane, swooping round the tables and catching Molly's head with a lowered arm as he passed.

'Gavin!' Shona barked at him. 'Leave her alone, you dickhead!'

'Gavin, *sit down*,' I commanded, hoping he'd actually do so. That wasn't a given – not at this time of day, at any rate. 'And Shona,' I added, 'it's nice to see you sticking up for Molly, but we don't name call in this classroom, okay?'

Happily, the other two boys appeared at that moment and, full of the gory details of some fight they had witnessed in the playground, were a timely distraction for the still pumped-up Gavin, so thankfully he did do as he was told. Which was a relief. When he was hyper like this it could sometimes take a good half-hour or more before he calmed down enough to be able to concentrate on anything. Which was bad for everyone else, of course, because his antics were so distracting.

What I had planned for this afternoon, however, might just distract him – and the others, too – in a more constructive way. Having chatted to Kelly, I'd decided to prepare the ground a little in readiness for Imogen's arrival. I'd therefore changed my scheduled task – which we could do instead once she joined us – for an activity that would celebrate difference.

I had already arranged the tables so they could all sit together, and once my coffee was made, and the tales of 'near death by the tennis courts' were out of the boys' systems, I called the children together and sat them down to explain the task.

'It's like art, isn't it, Miss?' Molly said. She was clearly proud to be the conveyor of a bit of inside information, bless her, though as soon as all eyes were on her she immediately blushed.

'It is, love,' I confirmed. 'But first I want you all to do some thinking. I want you to think about what it is that makes you different from everyone else.' I stopped then and dragged my old flip chart closer to the table, folding back the pages to reveal a blank one. I then took my marker pen. 'Here, see,' I said, as I began writing words on it. 'Here are some things that make me me. "Black hair",' I said, pointing. '"Small",' I added, writing it. '"Loud" ...'

This, predictably, got me a couple of snorts and giggles. 'All these things,' I went on, 'make me different from, say, Molly, who is nice and quiet – when she knows she should be – and has fair hair. Whereas Henry –' he straightened – 'Henry has something in common with me. Can you think what that might be?' I only waited a second before supplying the answer for them: 'He's also loud.'

More giggles, and I could see they had begun to work out what I was after. 'So what I'm going to do,' I said, 'is tear off a big sheet of paper for each of you, and you can put things on it that show all your differences. You can use the catalogues and scrap drawers if you want to cut things out and stick them on to brighten things up, but make sure you put your name across the top so we can tell who we're talking about when we pin them all up.

'After that,' I went on, 'we'll think of some really famous people, and how they're different, and some people who might have some kind of disability, and together we'll do some "difference" charts for them too. And that's because this week we're going to celebrate difference in a big way, and what's more –' I paused – 'I have a *prize* going begging. And it's going to the person who, by the end of the week, can show the best understanding of it, okay?'

As with any activity that involved cutting, sticking, mess-making and the possibility of a reward at the end of it, my young charges were immediately engaged. They were quick to set about gathering the materials they wanted to use for their creations and by the time I'd worked out the best area of wall to clear for the resultant works of art the room was buzzing with an air of productivity. It also gave me the chance to speak to them one-to-one, as I did every day, as well as their scheduled weekly half-hour life-space interviews. The few minutes in my corner were designed to give them a chance to let me know if there was anything that was troubling them, but today would also provide the perfect opportunity to prepare them individually for the arrival in the morning of our singular new pupil.

The children responded to news of Imogen pretty much as I'd expected. Molly, Shona and Ben all accepted her mutism without question, while Gavin and Henry were instantly curious.

'Why can't she speak?' Henry wanted to know. 'What happened to her voice? Did she get stabbed in the throat, Miss?'

I rolled my eyes. 'Of course not, silly,' I told him. 'There's nothing wrong with her throat. It's just that she can't speak.'

'So she must be a baby, then. Either that or a dummy,' he added disdainfully.

I skewered him on the end of one of my disapproving looks. 'Henry, what have we been talking about since you came back from lunch? *Difference*. All the things that make everyone different from everyone else. Your lovely strawberry blond hair, for example. Ben and Gavin don't have that, do they? And I bet they think your hair is far more interesting than theirs.'

'No they don't,' he huffed. 'They call me microphone head, Miss. Well, not no more, actually, 'cos I beat them to a pulp.'

I shook my head at the very young teenager sitting before me. The thing you couldn't miss about Henry travelled everywhere with him – that huge chip that was weighing down his shoulder, as the result of being at the bottom of such a big pile of brothers, and lacking any sort of father figure in his life. That and his hand-me-downs and general struggle to make his voice count at home sometimes made for a very angry young man.

I knew I was last-chance saloon where Henry was concerned. If he didn't change his fighting ways, he'd be permanently excluded, and I felt sorry for him. I had a bit of a soft spot for him too.

I looked at him now. 'Henry,' I chided, 'I know you didn't beat those boys up, just like I know that, being the oldest here, you're going to step up to the plate. You're going to help me, aren't you? Help make sure that Imogen doesn't get a hard time? Point out to the younger ones that she's just a little different – can you do that? I can count on you to do that for me, can't I?'

I watched Henry digest this and break into a grin. 'I can

be like your terminator, Miss, can't I? If the others pick on her I can zap them with my bionic arm, can't I? They'd soon stop saying stuff then, wouldn't they?'

I laughed. 'Er, I don't think I want you to be doing any zapping. But it would be a great help if you could just watch over her for a few days – you know, when I've got my back turned and stuff.'

This seemed to make him happy, because as he walked back to the group, his shoulders high, he announced that, as the oldest, he was officially looking out for the new girl. 'So no funny business,' he said, before turning back to me. Upon which he winked. I had to stop myself from laughing out loud.

Gavin's take on the apparent oddity was more practical. After a barrage of questions – Why couldn't she talk? Had she got ADHD? Was she 'on meds'? – he had the solution. 'You should give her some Ritalin,' he observed. 'That'll sort her out.'

One of my rules, given that I tended to spend my days with challenging children, was that easier-said-than-done-thing at the end of the working day of making a determined effort to take off my 'miss' hat and put on my 'mum' one.

I always smiled to myself at school when the kids them-selves found it difficult; when – at least at the beginning of the day, anyway – they would accidentally call me Mum instead of Miss. They'd always blush then, often furiously, but I took it as a compliment. I'd never wanted to be the sort of teacher who kept such a distance from their charges that it was a mistake that no child would ever make. Quite the contrary – I took these slips as evidence I was working in the right job; that I was someone they felt comfortable around. That was important – if they were comfortable enough to forget themselves around me then I would be in so much better a position to support them. Which could make the difference, in some cases, between returning to mainstream classes, back among peers, learning, and travelling even further down the road to isolation.

And I also knew that my drive to help them was partly as a consequence of seeing first hand how much that mattered, through helping Kieron with the many challenges of growing up with Asperger's.

Which he was still doing, as I observed when, letting myself into the house and slipping off my coat and shoes, it was to find him slumped on the sofa in front of the telly, as was currently his habit.

He was waiting, I knew. Waiting for me to come in and give him his tea, before Mike and Riley both got home from work. I went into the kitchen and pulled out a plate and some cutlery.

'Honestly,' I called to him as I dished out some casserole from the slow cooker, 'why you can't wait till the others get home is beyond me, Kieron. And if you can't wait, you could at least get off the sofa and help yourself to something.'

He looked across and gave me one of his pained looks as he turned down the TV volume. 'Oh, Mum,' he moaned. 'Don't get on at me. I'm stressed out enough as it is!'

'And what exactly have you got to be stressed about?' I asked him as I took the bowl of steaming casserole through to the dining-room table. I had strict rules about the eating of meals and where it was allowed to happen, even if I was generally a little on the soft side when it came to my son. 'Come on,' I said. 'Come through here and eat this before it gets cold. So, tell me,' I added as I set it down, and glancing at the evidence of a day spent mostly watching telly rather than career planning, 'have you thought any more about what you're going to do?'

Kieron scraped back a dining chair and plonked himself down wearily. 'Oh God, Mum,' he stropped. 'Five minutes you've been in and already you're getting on at me!'

I ruffled his hair and pulled a chair out. My cup of coffee could probably wait. 'Sorry, love,' I said. 'I don't want to get on at you. I want to *help* you. Dad and I were only saying this morning, perhaps we could sit down with you this evening – you know – go through some options with you maybe? It's no good for you, this – sitting around on your own all day, moping. You'll just get fed up, and you know what you're like – next thing, you'll end up getting in a state.'

He shovelled in a couple of mouthfuls before replying. He could eat for Britain could Kieron. 'I'm not in a state, Mum – I'm just bored. And I don't mean to snap. It's just that Jack and James and Si – they've got stuff going on, haven't they? Jack's got his new job, the others are at college …' He trailed off, and downed another mouthful. 'And it's like … well, it's like it's all right for them because they *know* what they're doing – and they know because they can all *do* stuff. But I can't. I don't think I can do anything that real grown-ups do. I'm crap at all that.'

'Nonsense!' I said firmly. It was a familiar refrain lately. As soon as he thought about the change inherent in making such big decisions, he took the safer route – putting it off for another day. 'Kieron,' I told him, 'you are not "crap", and of course you can do things.'

He could, too. Though his GCSE results had disappointed him, being mostly Ds, it wasn't as straightforward as it might have been. He'd struggled with dyslexia since primary school and his diagnosis of Asperger's had only come in the last two years, meaning valuable time and support that could have helped him achieve higher grades hadn't been available to him till much later in his school life. That he was capable of more wasn't in doubt – the teachers had all said so. I reiterated that fact again now. 'You can do anything you set your mind to,' I told him. 'You just have to decide what it is you *want* to do, that's all. And that's what you have to put your mind to – *deciding* – not avoiding. Which is why you and Dad and I need to sit down and have a proper talk. Anyway, right now I'm off upstairs to change and have a shower before they're back. And make sure you put that plate back when you're done, okay? *Okay?*'

'Um, oh, yeah. Will do,' he said, having, in typical teenage boy fashion, already tuned me out in favour of the bit of programme he could still see through the glass doors between the table and the telly.

Honestly, I thought to myself as I headed up the stairs, if anyone had told me when they were little that I'd be worrying about my kids so much at this age, I'd have thought they were mad. But of course, I'd been wrong –

older didn't necessarily mean less difficult to parent. It was just that you did your worrying on a different level.

But at least Kieron could communicate *his* worries – well, up to a point and after a fashion anyway. I thought back to the anxious-looking little girl who'd be joining my class the following morning. How could she be helped in her troubles – and she clearly had some troubles on her shoulder – if she couldn't communicate anything to anyone?

# Chapter 4

I was feeling lighter of heart as I walked into school the following morning, at least where Kieron was concerned. Where I had only prompted mild teenage disgruntlement, Mike had produced progress, and we'd all gone to bed with a plan that seemed workable – for Kieron to at least think about exploring the possibility of applying to the local college to do a two-year course in Media Studies, with an emphasis on music production.

It had been a friend of Mike's from work that had suggested it. His son had just finished one and had really enjoyed it, and, better still, it had clearly served him well. He was now doing an apprenticeship with a theatre group in London, learning how to produce music for shows.

Mike had done a soft-sell on it, knowing that to go in guns blazing would be likely to make Kieron anxious by default. Instead, he couched it in terms that made it sound more like a hobby he could dabble in than an actual college course. After all, he loved music as much as he loved football and superheroes (i.e. a *lot*), and once we looked into things further and found the teaching style was mostly small-group based, it began to seem much less daunting than he'd originally thought. He was still reticent, but he was also asking questions, at least, which was an encouraging development. But now came the biggie: his task for today was to take the bold and scary step of phoning the admissions office to try and make an appointment.

Whether he'd have managed it by the time I got home from work remained to be seen. I felt hopeful, though, and able to turn my attention to the probably equally scared young girl who was joining us today.

I could see Imogen and her grandmother when I walked into reception. They were seated in the corner, on the small sofa that was stationed there for the purpose, and both silently watched my progress through the double doors.

I was pleased to see they'd arrived early as it would be much less daunting for Imogen if she could come straight to my classroom with me than run the gamut of all the other kids arriving.

I raised an arm and waved. 'Morning!' I called to them, smiling. They both stood as I approached, as if to attention.

Mrs Hinchcliffe was holding Imogen's arm protectively, but it was clear she was keen to be gone. 'Do I have to stay with her?' she asked me, having acknowledged my greeting.

I shook my head. 'No, no, that's fine,' I told her. 'Imogen can come with me now.' I turned and met her gaze. 'Okay? And will you be picking Imogen up again?' I asked Mrs Hinchcliffe, 'or will she be making her own way home?'

Imogen's grandmother shuffled, a touch uncomfortably, I thought, before she answered. 'No,' she said, finally. 'She knows her way home. It's only five minutes away. And she won't want me here, I'm sure. Showing her up ...'

Now it was my turn to feel uncomfortable. It really did feel odd to be talking about this girl as if she was an inanimate object. 'Okay, then,' I said. 'Well, we'll be off then, shall we, Imogen? And I'll see you, well ... whenever, Mrs Hinchcliffe. Though it occurred to me that perhaps we could speak on the phone later – have a bit of a catch-up? If that's all right.'

She seemed a little surprised at my suggestion, but said that, yes, it would be fine, then headed back out into the warm autumn sunshine, throwing a 'Be good, Imogen' back towards us by way of a goodbye.

I'd already decided to skip my usual half-hour in the staffroom and as we were in school so early – there were still ten minutes to go till the bell went – take the opportunity to acclimatise Imogen to her new surroundings before the other children all came crashing in.

'Come on,' I told her now, beckoning her towards the doors to the main corridor. 'Follow me.'

She seemed reluctant to make eye contact, but fell into step with me, chin very firmly on chest. But not before I could see the strange blank expression that had now taken over her face. It really was mask-like; as if, now Nan had gone, a shutter had come down. It made the silence between us feel even more uncomfortable.

I chatted as we walked, trying to fill it. I told her about my own children, and how I would have been in school before her and her Nan were, had it not been for my daughter Riley and her scattiness in the mornings and how this particular morning she'd had us all in a spin, rushing around trying to find her a pair of her 'stupid' tights. I kept glancing at Imogen as I spoke, but it wasn't clear that she was even listening, since there was no response at all.

'There are going to be five other children joining us in a bit,' I went on. 'Three boys, two other girls – and they're all looking forward to meeting you. I think you'll like them – particularly the girls, Molly and Shona. They're a little younger than you – Shona's in year 8 but Molly's still in year 7 – and they're both lovely girls.'

The walk wasn't a long one, but it seemed so. It was a strange business, inanely chirping away to a girl who seemed not to want to listen or respond. And I wondered – what was going through her head right now? Still, my research had told me that this was the right thing to do – just keep on talking, even if it was into a void. And that, I thought, as we reached my classroom, I *was* good at.

'Here we are!' I said, as we approached the door. 'My little kingdom!'

It was something to see, too – a proper work of art. In contrast to every other classroom door in the school, mine was highly decorated; covered, top to bottom, in daffodils and daisies, all painted by various children who had passed through it and all cut out and covered in sticky-back plastic, in traditional *Blue Peter* style. A work of art in its own right, everyone in school commented on it, and I was pleased to see it prompt a reaction. No, not in words, but Imogen did seem to do a bit of a double-take on seeing it.

'We'll have to get you to paint a flower for it, too, eh?' I told her as I unlocked it. I laughed. 'I think there's just about room!'

Again, there was almost nothing in the way of a response, and it was an equally odd business trying to do my usual welcome spiel. I ushered Imogen to a seat, and as I proceeded to point out the various aspects of the classroom I felt increasingly like an air hostess – one who was trying to keep the attention of my single indifferent passenger, who only glanced up occasionally and apparently indifferently.

'And that door there,' I said, once I'd run through all the basic whats and wheres, 'is the emergency exit, as you can see, but we often take a table or two out there if the weather is nice. Might do today, in fact. We'll see …'

It was hard work, but just as I was wondering if I should next show her the brace position, I was rescued by the arrival of Henry.

'Morning, Miss!' he said brightly, grinning widely at the pair of us.

'I'm Henry,' he told Imogen with a confident can-do air. 'I came in early so I could check you were here. What's your name again?'

Meeting his eye now, Imogen seemed to physically shrink. Down went the head onto the chest, too.

41

'Her name is Imogen,' I reminded him. 'Imogen, Henry is our oldest. In fact he's your age, and he kind of helps me out, don't you, Henry? With some of the younger ones.'

I watched Henry swell with pride. 'Yeah, I do,' he confirmed. 'I make sure they don't mess about too much for Miss. An' I told them they gotta be all right with you, too. So they will be, okay?'

There was no response to this from Imogen, so I supplied one for her. 'Thanks, Henry,' I told him. 'And you're right. I'm sure they will be. Now, shall we get some drinks made before the others get here?'

Henry moved towards my little corner and grabbed the kettle so he could fill it for me. I was so impressed with him; was this the same boy who was an inch from exclusion? Maybe stewarding Imogen would be really good for him. 'Hot chocolate?' I asked Imogen. 'That's how we tend to start the day here. With a nice cup of hot chocolate and a biscuit.'

She glanced up and I noticed her gaze flutter up towards me. And was I mistaken or was that the trace of a smile? It was something, at any rate. Something we could build on. Perhaps we might be able to communicate after all. Right now, though, I took it as evidence that she would indeed like a hot chocolate, so I joined Henry and set about arranging all the plastic cups, plus my mug, ready for my next cup of coffee.

I'd done well with my hot-chocolate stash, which I'd shamelessly blagged not long after I'd arrived in the school. There was a drinks vending machine in the sixth-form block, and a man came every month to fill it, and one day, by chance, we'd met along one of the corridors and had fallen into conversation. I'd told him about how several of my kids came into school hungry and thirsty, and he'd told me about how a small proportion of the drinks had torn sleeves and couldn't go into the machines he serviced. They were usually thrown away, too. Would I like them?

It was a match made in heaven. I got a new supply of hot chocolate once a month, and he got a free cup of tea before he left and, more often than not, a biscuit as well.

It was a full ten minutes before the other kids arrived, and they were long ones, Imogen silently sipping her drink and Henry sneaking peeks at her as he did likewise. After his initial chattiness he didn't seem to know quite what to do now, and kept glancing towards the door, hoping for reinforcements. I think we were both relieved when a rumble in the corridor bore fruit and the other four kids came bowling in, Shona and Molly arm in arm as per usual, and Ben and Gavin doing their usual pushing and shoving.

'Ah,' I said, 'here's the rest of our little group, Imogen. Right,' I told them, 'come on in and take your seats everyone, and let's get this party started.'

I made quick introductions as I prepared chocolate for the rest, and told the girls to go and sit at Imogen's table. Today, with even numbers, we'd have a boys' group and a girls' group – for this morning's activity, at any rate. I also got out the biscuits, eyeing Ben as I always did. Ben, I knew, was one of the kids who never got breakfast, as his dad worked shifts and would be asleep when he'd left for school. I'd once asked him if he could maybe grab some toast to see him through, but his response was that there wasn't often any bread.

I couldn't think of Ben without feeling a sharp pang of sympathy, and today was no different. I glanced at him now, yawning away, looking as if he'd just tumbled out of bed fully clothed. His off-white shirt, unironed and crumpled, had its two bottom buttons missing, and was only half tucked into his grubby school trousers. He didn't have a school jumper, and when I'd asked him about that he'd told me it was because his dad didn't think it was worth spending the money as he'd probably be excluded soon and would be off to a different school.

'You can have one of my spares,' I'd said, this being the logical solution, but Ben, loyal to the last, and not wanting charity, shook his head. 'Thanks, Miss,' he'd said. 'But if my dad don't want me to have one then I won't have one.'

Free biscuits, however, were another matter – no one in my classroom ever seemed to turn them down and, though I could see Molly was embarrassed, listening to Shona trying to engage Imogen in conversation – she was blushing furiously – the atmosphere in the room wasn't quite as awkward as I'd feared.

And my plan for the morning would hopefully encourage that further.

'Right,' I said, once everyone had a drink and a biscuit. 'Chatter time is over. Time to listen.'

I handed out two packets of dried spaghetti and two bags of marshmallows, to the general appreciation of all concerned.

'Wobbly Towers!' said Henry as I did so. 'Yess!'

'Yes, Wobbly Towers,' I explained, for the benefit of Imogen and the others – Henry was the only one of the group who'd done the activity before, the other children having only been with me for a month or so. 'Henry's correct,' I said. 'That's what we're doing this morning. And today it's going to be boys against girls.'

I then went on to explain the basics of 'Wobbly Towers', one of my most popular and well-used group activities. I would give the children an hour, during which they had to spend half an hour designing and planning the structure of a wobbly tower, and then build one out of the sticks of dried spaghetti and the marshmallows. It was a little bit like creating the molecular structure models you'd see in science classes, but we made no mention of atoms and bonds or anything complex like that. They simply had to create something that would stand unsupported for at least one minute, with a prize going to the team who, in my 'professional' opinion, had been the most inventive with their construction ideas.

Wobbly Towers was a team activity, which meant it was also a great ice-breaker, which was why I did it so often. With children coming and going all the time it was important to plan activities that helped with the bonding process; especially important, given that the kids that came to me often did so because of their struggles to find friends.

Henry's hand shot up as soon as I'd finished speaking.

'Yes, Henry?' I said, one eye on Imogen's impassive face.

'Miss, do we get to eat the marshmallows after we've finished?'

'Hmm, let me think ...' I said, pretending to muse as I went to my desk to get paper and pencils for everyone. 'Well, if you take the full half hour to plan properly (the kids were always itching to plunge in impulsively and start building, so that was important) and if you do create a tower that stays upright for the whole minute ... then, yes, I suppose I could let you share the marshmallows out at the end.'

There were smiles all round. We had the same conversation, pretty much, every time we did it.

'Epic,' said Henry to his fellow boys, as they took the pieces of paper I was proffering. 'Let's show the girls, eh?'

Molly and Shona tutted as they came up behind them, Imogen falling into step behind Shona, and taking the paper and pencil she passed back to her.

'There we are,' Shona said to her. 'Just put your name at the top, seeing as how you don't like to talk. And Molly and me will tell you what you've got to write on it. Oh, and yes –' She turned to me. 'Miss, can I have another bit of paper? There,' she said, as I passed her another and she handed it over to Imogen. 'You can use *that* bit of paper to tell us stuff, can't you? It'll be like when I had tonsillitis and I lost my voice all day. I had to write everything down then, too.'

*Nice one, Shona!* I thought, as the children began to settle to their planning. What a clever, intuitive, emotionally intelligent girl she was. She would be okay, would Shona, I decided. Her late parents would have been so proud of her.

Which got me to thinking – what *was* the situation with Imogen's exactly? With the dad? The second wife? And where exactly was her mum? What precisely was the root of her current troubling situation? I would find out more about the family at some point, I imagined. But in the meantime, as of today, I was on a mission.

If there was no physical reason for Imogen's silence – and it seemed there wasn't – then my own mission, I decided, as the children set about their engineering one, was to find a way to *get* her to speak. To me.

# Chapter 5

Leaving the children occupied with their exciting engineering activity left me freed up to do a little more research. I'd already looked up the basics of selective mutism on the internet, and everything I'd discovered so far had told me pretty much the same thing: that children with the condition 'opted out' of speaking in social situations – of which school was an obvious example. Most of the time, however, they spoke completely normally in close family environments, when no one else was listening – as in at home.

I wasn't sure about that key phrase 'opt out', though. It seemed to me – again, reading the research I had come across – that it wasn't a case of a child 'opting' not to speak, but rather of them literally being unable to do so. In fact, another thing I learned was that children found it so distressing that they would actively avoid situations which would bring on their mutism. And, unfortunately, you couldn't avoid school.

But where had it come from? In Imogen's case, what had been the trigger? That there had been one didn't seem to be in doubt. So it was a case of going back, then – back in time to look at the history. Because if I could tease out what had caused it, I had the best tool to help her. Without knowing it, we wouldn't be addressing the problem – only the symptoms. Simple logic, but it seemed the best place to start.

My session on the computer done, I sat at my desk and watched Imogen intently. Shona, ever the mother hen, bless her, was doing her best to take charge of their little group. And, taking her lead, Molly seemed to be adapting to their unusual situation, understanding the need to provide a commentary, to compensate for the lack of recip- rocation when either of them spoke to our newest Unit 'recruit'. 'That's right, Imogen,' she was saying, 'Shona meant to criss-cross the straws there, just like you've drawn them. Well done.'

I had to smile. If you'd witnessed it cold you'd imagine they were speaking to a much younger child. But Imogen didn't seem to mind. In fact, her expression, usually so deadpan, seemed to soften now the girls were clucking and fussing so much around her. Was that it? Did she lack attention? Feel excruciatingly self-conscious? It was so hard to fathom someone who didn't speak. All those little clues. It wasn't just what children had to say to you that mattered – you learned so much just from the *way* they spoke, too.

I was just pondering our little enigma when Kelly breezed in, beaming smiles for all, as per usual. Imogen glanced up, but I noticed she took very little interest. Not anxious, not nervous, not stressed by a new person. Perhaps shyness wasn't a factor here at all.

'You must have read my mind,' I told Kelly, standing up to pop the kettle on for coffee. 'I could actually do with nipping to the staffroom – got to make a phone call. If you're free to hang around for a bit, that is.'

Kelly nodded. 'If you'll throw a chocolate digestive into the deal, I'll happily stay,' she said. 'I'm free till lunchtime as it happens. All yours.'

I gave Kelly a quick update on what the children were up to and, before I left, sensing that I ought to let Imogen know what I was doing, went across to the girls' table to let her know.

'This is looking good,' I told them all, looking at the planning notes they'd made already, then, lowering my voice, said, 'You know, you might have a good chance of winning, girls. And, Imogen, your handwriting's really neat.'

There was no reply from her, obviously, but I saw that same flutter of recognition that she'd understood and was pleased with what I'd said. What could it be like, I wondered, to have that barrier between yourself and the world? Did she want to respond, formulate an answer, yet be physically unable to deliver it, or was it a more conscious thing? What a curious thing it was. Particularly since she spoke normally at home.

Mrs Hinchcliffe didn't seem particularly pleased to hear from me. In fact I got the impression as soon as she answered the phone that despite my having already mentioned that I'd like to, she felt my calling her was somehow irregular. I assured her that wasn't the case; that, where practical, it was an important part of my role to try and work in co-operation with a child's parents or guardians, to give them the best chance to deal with whatever their particular problems were and help ease them back into mainstream life in school.

'Well, I don't know that there's much I can tell you,' she said. 'She was living with her dad before, as you know, and having lots of problems at her old school. Bullying, teasing, that sort of thing.'

'Just her and Dad, then?' I asked. 'What about Mum?'

I heard her sigh. 'No, no,' she said. 'I told you, Imogen lived with my son. It had just been the two of them since her mother walked out on the pair of them …'

'Oh, dear. I'm sorry to hear that.'

'Yes, well …' said Mrs Hinchcliffe. 'Believe me, you don't know the …' And then she checked herself. She was clearly anxious not to be indiscreet. 'And they were fine …'

'So does Imogen see her mum at all?'

'No, she doesn't. Not at the moment.' I could hear the edge in Mrs Hinchcliffe's voice still. 'She's been getting settled into her new life, and – well – it's not really for me to say, Mrs Watson. It's none of my business, is it?'

The implication being that it was none of mine either. But yes, it *was* her business. It was certainly her business. She was the one holding the flipping baby, wasn't she?

'I suppose not,' I said anyway, because I didn't want to antagonise her. What I really wanted to ask next was why *he* wasn't bringing up his daughter. There must have been

Casey Watson

a reason, after all. But that would only antagonise Mrs
Hinchcliffe further, I didn't doubt, especially as I was fast
getting the impression that my line of enquiry was one that
wasn't really considered relevant. I was being fed the line
that it was bullying at school that had prompted Imogen's
selective mutism – but what about her mum? Might her
absence from Imogen's life have some bearing? I tried to
imagine how Kieron or Riley might have coped if I'd disappeared suddenly from *their* lives – and I couldn't. Losing a
mother was a *huge* thing. Surely it must have contributed?

I took another tack. 'So, Dad – your son – he's on his
own now, then, is he?'

'No, not at all,' said Mrs Hinchcliffe. 'Graham has a new
partner. Lovely girl, she is. That poor woman,' she said
with sudden animation. 'It's a lot to take on for anyone,
isn't it? Someone else's child. And what with Graham working away …'

'Oh,' I said. 'He works away, does he?'

'He's a coach driver, dear,' she said. 'European tours.
Luxury ones …' And with the emphasis on the 'luxury' bit.
I could hear the pride in her voice.

'Oh, I see,' I said. 'So his other half has to –'

'His *wife*. Gerri, her name is. Lovely girl. Tried everything, she has, and – well, I'm sure you know how difficult
children can be these days,' she huffed. 'It's a miracle she
didn't walk out on him as well, frankly. Never stood a
chance with Imogen, she didn't. Not a chance. That's why
we've got her. I mean, what choice do we have? And she
doesn't see it, of course …'

'What, your daughter-in-law?'

'No! *Imogen!* No idea of the sacrifices her father's made for her. She really hasn't. I mean it's her mum she should be bearing a grudge towards – I mean, anyone would say the same, wouldn't they? Upping and leaving them like that. It's not her dad she should be taking it out on, is it? I keep trying to tell her that, Mrs Watson. I mean, at least he flipping *stayed* with her … And poor Gerri. I've never known anyone so selfless. She's the patience of a saint, that one. But, no … she can't see that. Can't see what's plain as the nose on her face, that one.'

Mrs Hinchcliffe sighed again then, an exasperated sigh, and I got a strong impression that here was a lady who probably loved her grandchild dearly, but was emotionally exhausted with having so much responsibility on her shoulders, and at a loss to know what to do with Imogen by now. I also got the feeling that she was caught between two stools. I had the impression she was not only trying to be a good grandmother but a good mother, too. Taking the strain off her son. And perhaps a bit too much?

And what did she mean by 'never stood a chance'? I decided not to press the point, however. 'Oh dear,' I said. 'That's sad. They don't get along, then? Do you think that's a factor in the mutism? Or did it start earlier? Some time after mum and dad split up, perhaps?'

But Mrs Hinchcliffe was having none of it. 'No, I *told* you. It was that *school*. She was fine after the break-up. Well, not completely fine, obviously – would *you* be fine if your mother just upped sticks and left you? I imagine not, Mrs Watson. But she was still speaking. No, it was that dreadful school that did it – useless, they were. All the name-calling – because of her hair, because of her freckles, because of her mum having left – you name it.'

'Children can be so cruel, can't they?'

'Oh, indeed they can, Mrs Watson. I don't doubt you've seen plenty of that sort of thing for yourself. Just plain *nasty*. That's when she shut down. And can you blame her? But she's got to learn to deal with it, hasn't she? She needs toughening up a bit. That's what my husband says, and I agree with him. Needs to learn how to shrug it off more.'

There was another clear picture emerging; that of a rather 'old school' kind of grandad. A man keen to raise his granddaughter in a 'no-nonsense' kind of way. The type for whom the 'let's talk about it' approach was probably anathema.

'Perhaps,' I said carefully, 'and perhaps the bullying *was* a trigger. From the research I've done on selective mutism, it seems there *is* usually a specific trigger, as I said … How is she at home? I mean, I know you say she talks normally there, but aside from that, how does she seem? More confident? More relaxed?'

'Oh, she's certainly confident. You probably think she's quite a quiet girl from what you've seen of her so far.'

Mrs Hinchliffe was right, there. No doubt about it. I agreed I did.

'But she isn't at all, you know. Shouts and screams at us – and for no apparent reason half the time, either. Sullen, too. Things don't go her way, don't we know about it! It's no wonder her dad and step-mum needed a break!'

Something occurred to me. 'What about Dad? I'm assuming they speak on the phone. Do they?'

'Oh, no – she won't speak to her father. Punishing him, is what we think. And the psychologist woman does, too. Won't say a word to him. Calls all the time – of course he does. But nothing. Like I said, it's *us* she takes it out on.'

'I'm really sorry to hear that,' I sympathised, 'and you're quite right, she's not come over like that at all. Mind you, lots of children play out their frustrations in either one place or the other. I've seen lots of that – as well as plenty of kids who are naughty in school but absolute angels at home.' I paused then. 'Speaking of which,' I added, having sensed we were at what seemed the perfect moment, 'I'd love to come and visit you all at home – you know, try to get a fuller picture of what we're dealing with. Do you think we could arrange that?'

'At home?' Mrs Hinchcliffe paused. 'Well, I suppose so. If you think it might help. Though I'd have to ask my husband first, of course.'

'Of course,' I said. 'Of *course* you must. So how about you do so, and then get back to me …'

'What, call up the school and leave a message?'

'Yes, that would be perfect,' I said. 'I'd really appreciate that, Mrs Hinchcliffe. Oh, and one thing – it would be best if you didn't mention anything about it to Imogen beforehand. If she knows in advance that I'm popping round she might get nervous, mightn't she? Whereas if I just arrive, she's more likely to be at her most normal.'

'And it's normal, this, is it?' she asked. 'You know – you coming round visiting people's houses?'

I wondered if there was an edge of reluctance in her voice. But no, I didn't think so; she'd not been slow in airing her feelings once she'd got going, after all. No, she just genuinely didn't imagine people from schools did such a thing. Probably the legacy of her husband's 'old-school' ideas.

'Yes, it is,' I reassured her. 'All part of my role in pastoral care. Where a child has difficulties – well, I'm sure we're all after the same thing, aren't we? To get to the root of it, and work together to find a solution.'

'Well that would *certainly* be nice,' Mrs Hinchcliffe agreed. And I could tell how wholeheartedly she meant it.

'Ah, Mrs Watson,' Kelly enthused, when I returned to my classroom 20 minutes later, 'take a look at these beauties. You certainly have some talent in this room of yours!'

'Wow,' I said, circling both tables, the children standing aside proudly to let me inspect their creations. I was pleased to notice that while Henry, predictably, was holding up the tower on the boys' table, it was Imogen who had a steadying hand on the girls' creation. 'These are spectacular,' I told them all, 'and, looking at all your planning notes' – I paused here to check both sets – 'also almost exactly as you'd originally envisioned them. Excellent. I tell you what,' I finished, 'I think I am going to find it almost impossible to pick a winner today.'

Ben coughed then, to get my attention. 'Miss,' he suggested, eyeing up the remaining marshmallows, 'we were thinking. If it's too hard to pick, and you think we're all winners, instead of giving one group a prize we could just share the rest of the marshmallows, couldn't we?'

I grinned at Kelly, who I didn't doubt had already heard

this line of thinking. 'What do you think, Miss Vickers? Do we think they all deserve to win?'

'You know,' said Kelly, 'I think I do. In fact, I'd had another thought. Since we've already taken photos of both towers for the evidence board, I was thinking we could sabotage these wonderful creations and eat the lot.'

The whole group exploded into gleeful shouts of 'Yes!' and, once again, I was pleased to note, this included Imogen. Not with her voice, perhaps, but definitely with her small but encouraging grin. She might not be speaking, I thought, but she was definitely engaging.

'Oh, go on then,' I said. 'Just make sure you save me a pink one.'

The unexpected bounty at the end of our session of Wobbly Towers set the tone for the remainder of the morning. Had anyone glanced in at my classroom before lunch that day, they could be forgiven for wondering quite why the Unit was known as the place where the most challenging children went to. Or, indeed, quite what they did all day – apart from laughing and scoffing marshmallows, that was.

It was one reason why the evidence board, which we updated with their planning notes and photographs as soon as the marshmallows were gone, was so important. Not only did it provide the children with much-needed evidence of how much they had achieved during their time with me, it also proved to the teachers and other staff members that the children were actually learning something curriculum-related, rather than being just in some sort of behaviour-management holding pen. Hard though it might have been for me to believe when I first started, a few – naming no names, of course – really did seem to see it as some sort of cop-out: a sin-bin where kids came for punishment and didn't do very much in the way of school work. Finally, it helped *me*, in that it gave me the opportunity to assess which lessons worked well and which didn't. I was learning too, and I could usually tell by the standard of work my kids produced whether the children had enjoyed it and also, most importantly, benefited from it.

At lunchtime the boys, as usual, were first to the door – out of the blocks, like 100-metre sprinters, it often seemed; with a sixth sense for the first tinkling of the bell. I felt slightly guilty that they'd stuffed down a fair few marshmallows each before lunch, but didn't doubt they'd find room for dinner too.

The girls, on the other hand, lingered. I'd already been so impressed with Shona and Molly this morning, and here they were again, thinking about Imogen's needs; and I realised that rather than just disappear off to the lunch hall without her they were waiting for me to tell them what to do.

'Imogen,' I said, 'would you like to come down to lunch with me?' It was an offer I'd make to any new pupil, disorientated and nervous as they'd invariably be.

Imogen glanced towards Shona before casting her gaze down.

'You can go with Miss if you want,' Shona told her. 'Or you can come with me an' Molly.' She put an arm around her waist – a friendly gesture that was so typical of her. 'If you wanna come with us, just nod, and if you don't, that's okay. You can go with Miss and she'll look after you instead.'

Imogen's nod was almost immediate, and before I could add anything further the three of them were already half-way out of the classroom.

''Bye then, girls,' I said, then, turning to Kelly, mouthed 'wow'.

'A turn-up for the books,' she agreed, once the girls had disappeared off down the corridor.

'Not that I'm counting my chickens,' I said, 'but bloody hell – what about Shona today? So maternal, bless her. Maybe she'll be the key to unlocking whatever Imogen has locked in.'

That and that home visit, I remembered. Which it seemed was definitely going to happen, Donald passing on the news, once I'd gone up for some lunch myself, that the Hinchcliffes were happy for me to visit at 5 p.m. that Thursday.

Though, with the afternoon going as productively as the morning had before it, by home time I was even beginning to wonder if Imogen might speak sooner rather than later, after all. Perhaps I'd been pessimistic. Perhaps it wouldn't be too long.

Perhaps it would turn out that in my head I'd been making a mountain out of a molehill. We would see. It was a nice thought, at least.

# Chapter 6

My optimistic mood took me all the way home and, as I got inside and saw the enormous grin on Kieron's face, I had an inkling it might be set to continue.

'Here, let me get that, Mum,' he said, rushing to help me pull my large satchel off my shoulder and relocate it to the back of one of the dining-room chairs. The teachers mostly carried briefcases but I rather liked my school bag. It might have seemed sentimental – and maybe it was – but it was also very practical.

'Thanks, love,' I said gratefully. 'And what's the grin for?'

It grew wider still. Kieron was obviously bursting to tell me something. 'It's because I have big news!' he beamed.

I rolled my sleeves up and headed towards the kitchen to put the kettle on and start on tea. 'Big news, eh?'

'Very big news,' he confirmed, following me in there. 'You know Si, my mate.'

'Indeed I do,' I said, nodding. I would do, after all. They'd been in nursery school together.

'Well, he's changed his course at college. He was doing some sports science course, but he wasn't really enjoying it, so they let him change it. To that one Dad was talking about – you know? That Media Studies thing, or whatever it is. Anyway, Si loves it. And from what he's told me, it sounds well good.'

I smiled as I rummaged in the fridge to check out the options. For Kieron to think something was 'well good' meant it was borderline spectacular. He wasn't one for bestowing compliments lightly. 'Does it now?' I said, rising. 'So what's it to be? Spag bol or sausages?'

'Mum!' he said, rolling his eyes. 'Are you even listening? I'm talking about my future here, you know. It's really important!'

'Of course I'm listening,' I told him. 'I'm just multi-tasking, love. It's what we women do best. And I'm hearing that the course Dad told you about the other day seems much more appealing now that Simon is already on it – have I got that bit right? And the next bit is that because of that you've decided you're going to give it a go yourself, yes?'

Kieron looked at me open-mouthed. 'Who are you?' he said incredulously. 'Derren Brown or something? You just read my mind!'

I grinned. 'Derren Brown is a magician, sweetie, not a mind-reader. But, yes, I reckon I did, right?'

I gave him a hug. I was playing it cool, but this was the best news imaginable. All he had to do now was actually follow through. 'I am so proud of you, love,' I said, 'and I'm sure it will really suit you. So. Have you phoned up and asked if there's actually a place left on it for you?'

It seemed it was Kieron's turn to do a bit of mind-reading. 'I knew you'd ask that,' he said. 'And I've beaten you to it, as it happens. I've done even better. I've been down there with Si and I've filled all the forms in and everything. And even though I've already missed the first fortnight – *obviously* – they told me that's okay because I can just catch up. Oh, and I can start there tomorrow! Well, as long as I take in my passport, that is. Where *is* my passport? I've been looking for it but I can't find it anywhere.'

Now it was *my* jaw hanging open. I yanked it back into position. Then sent up a quick prayer of gratitude for there being a friend called Si in this world.

'That's amazing,' I said. 'Fabulous news, love! Now I feel even prouder. And don't worry about your passport. Dad will have just put it somewhere safe. And you know what? I think we'll forget cooking and order in pizzas for tea, to celebrate. Like the sound of that?'

He liked the sound of it very much. There was still the small matter of actually finding his passport – Kieron didn't like holidays so we tended not to do them, and I knew dinner wouldn't happen till the offending article had been tracked down – but, all in all, it was definitely a cause for celebration. Whenever Kieron was upset or stressed, it played out in all sorts of little ways, which couldn't help but have an effect on the rest of us, so I knew Mike and Riley would be up for a celebration as well. Plus no one in our house *ever* said no to a big slab of take-away pizza. What kind of normal person would, after all?

My working day, in contrast, was invariably far from 'normal'. Work, for me, usually meant taking a deep breath and preparing for the unexpected. That was the central irony of working in the sort of unit I did. That what was designed to be a place of calm, routine and order for the kids that came *to* me, was, in terms of teaching strategies and decisions about how to handle conflicts and flare-ups, also a place where two days were never going to be the same.

My current six – Molly and Shona, Gavin, Henry and Ben, and, of course, now Imogen – seemed, in my short experience, to represent a fairly standard spread. Some the bullied, some the bullies, all of them united in their need to be heard and understood, and then carefully managed, and helped to re-integrate where possible.

And, by and large, I had a handle on them both as individuals and collectively, and sufficient strategy to see the way ahead. By that Thursday, however – the day of my meeting with Imogen's grandparents – I was beginning to realise that understanding Imogen was going to be particularly tricky. How could you hear a child who didn't speak? And if she didn't talk, how could you get to know her? As for understanding her – well, I was closer to taking wing and flying round the playground.

I was also aware that Imogen was beginning to disassociate from the group. Poor Molly and Shona were trying their best but I could see they were beginning to flag now.

There was only so much you could do when you weren't getting any feedback. The boys, equally dispiritingly, were off on another tack altogether. Having clearly reached the conclusion that ignoring her was boring, they had started to tease her about both her silence and her hair colour – particularly Gavin.

'Why don't you whinge like all the other girls?' he wanted to know as he raced round and round the girls' table, like a Duracell bunny, his Ritalin having obviously been administered a little on the late side today. 'I know why!' he added, grinning at his own powers of deduction. 'It's because if you did you'd be a ginger whinger, that's what you'd be!'

'Gavin!' I said, making a beeline for him, brows knitted. 'Please go and sit in the reading area and wait quietly for me. You know we don't tease others in here, don't you? Now, go on, off to the book corner and choose a book, please.'

I underlined this instruction with a bit of firm, purposeful guidance, which he didn't resist. He never did. He was just like the human equivalent of one of those bouncy rubber superballs, which boinged around in whichever direction they were sent.

My book corner was a godsend, simple though it was. And it was simple; just two bookcases, set at right angles to form an L shape, but with the book side facing inwards, towards the corner. This meant it created a cosy, square-shaped area in a previously unused corner and, with the addition of a square of old carpet and a selection of bean bags and cushions, a place where children like Gavin could have a separate and solitary place to calm down.

'I was only messing, Miss!' he protested, as he invariably did. 'I don't want to sit on my own!'

'Well, you should have thought about that, shouldn't you?' I said, pointing back towards a gloomy-looking Imogen. 'Ten minutes, then you can come back out and apologise to Imogen for being so thoughtless towards her.'

Gavin scowled. 'Why should I, Miss? What's the point?' he huffed. 'She never speaks to me, so why should I be made to speak to her?'

I was expecting the usual giggles – Gavin always liked to work an audience – but on this occasion, perhaps because they'd noticed my expression, they refrained and looked on silently while I pointed again to the corner, and Gavin, knowing the game was up, slunk behind the shelves out of sight.

I went back to my desk. Of course, there could be another reason for his classmates' silence. It could equally be that he was beginning to get on their nerves, just as he had in his mainstream classes. I made a mental note to speak to his parents about his medication. He was supposed to be with me for just a term, while he got used to it, but it was crucial that he took it at the same time each morning, as well as early enough for it to have kicked in by the time he arrived in school.

There would seem to be no such practical solutions for Imogen, however, who I decided to keep a close eye on throughout the day, in preparation for my visit to her home later. With Shona really her only anchor among her eccentric little bunch of classmates, I noticed she was following her almost every move, so it would be interesting to see how she approached the task I had planned for the morning – whether she'd come up with her own ideas or just do what she mostly had being doing: letting someone else be the one who led the way.

We were working, as we often did, on conflict resolution. And having first resolved the earlier conflict between Imogen and Gavin (up to a point, anyway; he mumbled a sorry and she said nothing), it seemed the perfect time. Conflict resolution was a big part of what we did in the Unit, and not only as a consequence of day-to-day squabbles. We actively included it in the curriculum as well, because it was a big part of the reason why the kids we worked with needed to be with us; they had insufficient strategies to deal with the many conflicts an average day in a child's life could throw up. It was drama based, and required teamwork, which meant collaboration and discussion – again, things that we worked hard to encourage.

The activity took the form of a comic strip, which had the normal run of pictures, but no dialogue; it was the children's job to decide who said what and when. The scene was classroom-based, starting with a frustrated-looking teacher standing at a blackboard, glowering as two of her pupils were obviously arguing with one another, while the rest of the class all looked on.

The idea was that the children had to decide what was happening and plan two short plays around it, one with what they considered to be a 'good' outcome, and one where the outcome was 'bad'. They would then perform both plays, and I'd film as they were doing so, in order that we could all watch and discuss the plays afterwards.

This sort of exercise was helpful for two reasons. It was obviously a good way for them to practise skills such as listening and negotiating, as well as making them think about such concepts as a 'moral code'. But it was also helpful for me, being a chance to get to know what made their minds work; seeing what they'd come up with in terms of solutions without any influence from me.

I got them started, then went over to my desk, ostensibly to do some paperwork but partly so that I could watch them discreetly. I was particularly interested in how Imogen might be allocated a part in the finished plays.

And I was looking forward to seeing what they came up with. What I hadn't figured on, however, was that Shona might be having a bad day.

With the children planning quietly, and mostly harmoniously, I was browsing the internet for Shakespeare quotes when I heard Shona's raised voice. 'No!' she snapped. 'Why does it have to be *that*?'

I looked up to see her looking daggers at Henry.

'Because, Miss Bossy Boots, that's what we chose!' he shouted back.

I noticed Imogen, who'd seemed reasonably engaged up to that point, shrink back into her 'closed' posture and hang her head. It was a very clear gesture. She was keeping well out of it. Ironic that it was meant to be a lesson on conflict resolution, I thought, as I watched and waited to see what would happen. Hang your head, shut your mouth. Don't get involved.

'Well, if I'm meant to be the teacher,' Shona shot back, 'I should be allowed to pick what lesson I'm teaching! And

I'm not doing a stupid "boys" lesson! There's no such thing, anyway! No one has lessons about cars, you idiot!'

Henry, another strong personality, wasn't about to give in, though. 'We can say it's a *project*!' he retaliated, sneering at her as if to say that anyone with half a brain would have known that. 'And anyway, it's three against two, so that's what we're doing. You can't always have it your own way, Shona. It's not fair!'

Things were definitely escalating, but I think everyone in the room was taken aback when Shona leapt from her chair, knocking it back onto the floor, and lunged for a startled Henry, fists flying.

She was already hammering at him, swinging punches, by the time I'd got up and come round from the other side of my desk, sobbing and calling him names as she did so.

'What the hell?' Henry yelled as he tried to protect himself from Shona's blows. 'Miss, she's mental! Miss! Get her off me!'

'Shona,' I said firmly, rushing to get to her and pull her away, 'what on earth is the matter? What's brought this on?'

I had to keep a firm grip on her wrists to keep her from wriggling from my grasp. She was surprisingly strong, and very, very angry. 'Let me go!' she screamed. 'I'm going to kill him! I swear I am, Miss – I *hate* him!' And I didn't doubt she'd have inflicted damage had I not been able to keep that grip on her, before twisting her around so that she was facing me and bending down to be more at her level. 'Shh,' I soothed. 'Shh, Shona. Calm down a minute, will you? What's wrong? What's made you so angry?'

She stopped struggling then. Went limp, in fact. She wasn't the sort of child who regularly flew into uncontrollable rages, I didn't think, and having just done so it was as if she had shocked herself more than anyone. She certainly seemed to mentally gather herself together. I felt her relax under my grip and risked letting her go. She didn't move. 'Well?' I asked her gently.

She looked at me, her eyes full of tears as yet unshed. 'I don't know, Miss,' she said in a small voice. 'I don't feel very well. Could I go and sit in the corner with books for a bit?'

She was certainly red in the face. I felt her forehead. It was a little warm, though that might have just been the physical exertion. 'Do you want to go to the medical room for a bit instead?' I suggested. 'Or shall I have someone go and tell the office to call home for you?'

The tears welled in her eyes and I could have kicked myself as soon as I'd spoken. Why had I said 'home'? What an idiot! That word would have been such an emotive one for her. Since the death of her parents in a road accident, she had no 'home', did she? She was currently billeted with her aunt and uncle and cousins. So, yes, *their* home, but not the home *she'd* always known. It all seemed so obvious, then. Of course she didn't want to make the lesson about cars.

I quickly put my arm around her and steered her to the place she wanted to go; the place where she could compose herself in private. 'That's fine, love,' I said briskly, knowing that to sympathise too much would only make things worse for her. 'You go ahead. Have a sit down and read a book. You can skip this lesson if you like.'

Henry puffed out his chest at this, looking positively indignant. 'What!' he squeaked. 'She doesn't even get *done* for that? Oh my God – if that had been me, I'd have been excluded or something, for definite. Oh. My. *God!*'

'That's *enough*, Henry,' I said firmly, anxious to nip any outbursts from him in the bud. The truth was that if it *had* been, he might well have been right. Henry only had so much rope left to play with in school, and I didn't want my classroom to be the place where it ran out.

'Right,' I said more generally. 'This was obviously a bad idea today. Change of plan. You can all get out your workbooks and write your own versions of the script. I'll read them all at lunchtime and choose the one we're going to act out this afternoon, once everyone has had a chance to calm down.'

There was a small rumbling of dissent, mostly, but not exclusively, from Henry, but it soon settled. No earthquake today.

'Come on, Imogen, you too,' I said gently as I passed her. 'You can be one of the quiet ones in the play, if you like,' I added, 'the sensible one who keeps out of the argument, eh?'

I had hoped to see a flicker of a smile, but it didn't happen, and by the time I had returned to my desk I noticed that, although she had at least opened her workbook, she'd still made no move to pick up her pen.

But perhaps that was it, I thought, mindful of poor Shona, holed up with a paperback, and who I'd need to have a chat to when the bell went. Perhaps conflict-resolution exercises were still a step too far for my current charges. I glanced again at Imogen. And perhaps for this one in particular. After all, she already had a resolution to whatever conflicted her. Say nothing.

Well, it *was* a strategy, I supposed. Least said soonest mended? Perhaps this afternoon I'd be some way to finding out.

# Chapter 7

Lunchtime seemed to fly by with a speed all of its own. They often did if you let class time spill over after the bell went, and, by the time I'd read through the scenarios the children had written and given to me, 20 minutes had already been gobbled up.

Putting the workbooks down, I decided I'd zip up to the staffroom to see if Kelly was free to assist during the afternoon session. When you were doing something that was both physical *and* creative, I'd learned, it always paid to have a second pair of adult hands, to help manage any hotheads and artistic differences.

But on my way there I remembered that I'd planned to look in on Gary Clark, too, and should perhaps do that first, as it was on the way.

Gary was the school's Child Protection Officer, or CPO. He was based in our school but also worked with all the feeder primary schools in the area, as well as doing home visits and dealing with issues such as truancy. He also ran teacher-training sessions on emotional literacy; something the government were becoming increasingly keen for schools to foster, a child's emotional well-being being as important, they were realising, as their academic potential.

Protocol dictated that I let Gary know if I was planning to do a home visit, such as I was going to do today after school. He was a lovely man with a calm outlook on everything. In his mid-forties and a dress-down-rather-than-up type of person, he was very easy to get along with and it seemed that all the children thought so too. I already knew he had been as interested in finding out more about Imogen's selective mutism as I had, because Don had already told me. In fact, one of the first things Gary told me when I showed up in his office was that he'd already arranged for a clinician to come into the school the following Monday to give us a little more insight into the condition.

'And it turns out that there are apparently several types of SM,' he told me, 'all of which can stem from different triggers. So it's not a "one size fits all" kind of thing.'

'That's interesting,' I said, 'because nothing I've seen on the internet so far really seems to fit where Imogen's concerned, so it would be really valuable to get the insight of an expert.'

'Let's hope it's helpful, then,' he said. 'And I was just on my way down to find you and tell you, funnily enough. So you've saved me a journey. For which extremely grateful thanks. If I'm lucky, I might still be in time for whatever delights cook has whistled up in the dining room.'

'Hmmph,' I said. 'Lunch? Chance would be a fine thing. Have you seen Kelly, by the way? I need to see if she's free p.m.'

'She'll be in the staffroom, I imagine. Last time I saw her she was heading rapidly in that general direction. Clutching a bag that looked suspiciously like it came from the local bakers. If you're quick you might be in with a shout at getting a muffin …'

Leaving Gary to grab his jacket, I set off myself, immediately bumping into Shona, who was standing leaning against the corridor wall.

'Oh, hi, sweetheart,' I said. 'Were you waiting to see Mr Clark?' She shook her head. 'I wanted to see you,' she said, 'and Mr Dawson said he'd seen you go in here … If that's all right?' she hurriedly added. 'Imogen's okay, and everything. She's in the playground with Molly.'

I was touched by her rush to reassure me, but also concerned that Shona had taken it upon herself to be Imogen's guardian to the extent that she thought I'd tell her off for not being at her side every single minute; if so, she was taking on a responsibility too far.

Gary joined us in the corridor. 'D'you want to use my office?' he said, gesturing back inside, obviously having heard us. 'I've got some photocopying and stuff to do so I won't be rushing back.'

I smiled gratefully. 'That would be lovely, Mr Clark,' I said, motioning to Shona that she should go in. 'Might just pinch a couple of your biscuits, too. I seem to have forgotten about eating lunch today.'

We exchanged a smile and I followed Shona in. I was

glad to see her looking better after her unexpected outburst of the morning. Unexpected, I judged, by her as much as me.

'Are you doing okay, love?' I asked her, grabbing a spare chair rather than heading behind Gary's enormous desk. I'd struggle to see over the piles of paperwork in any case.

She nodded. 'I'm okay, Miss. I just wanted to say I'm sorry.'

'Sorry?' I said. 'Sweetheart, it's me that should be saying sorry. I should have realised, shouldn't I? I don't think Henry knew for a moment the he'd be upsetting you, do you? But cars are going to be the last thing you want to talk about, aren't they? It must have been very upsetting.'

I paused to let her speak, but she didn't. It often worked that way. Kids came to talk, but when they got to it they couldn't. Not at first. 'Though, you know,' I added, 'you don't have to talk about it if you don't want to.'

Shona sighed. 'I know he didn't do it on purpose, Miss. But … but, it's just that sometimes I get so tired of feeling like I do. I mean, my auntie and uncle are lovely, but … it's just, well, there's my little cousins, and I feel terrible if I cry in front of them, because they start crying then as well, and my auntie … she cries sometimes, because she misses mummy too, and I feel bad about that as *well*, and that makes me want to cry more and … it's just … it's just so hard, Miss, trying to pretend you're not upset when you are.'

The sadness in the room felt almost touchable. It was a terrible thing to have happened and it couldn't be undone. The poor child had such an unbearable weight on her shoulders, it didn't bear thinking about, really.

'Oh, love, I *do* know. I know exactly what you mean. It's horrible feeling you have to bottle your feelings up all the time, isn't it? Tell me, are you still seeing your bereavement counsellor?' She nodded. 'And are they helping?'

'Kind of,' Shona said. 'I just …' I could see her chin beginning to wobble. 'It's just that I wish I knew how long it'll be before it stops feeling like this. I just feel so sad. I miss my mummy so much, and my dad, and I …' She could no longer speak now and instead let out a huge racking sob. One that tore at my heart as I pulled her into my arms.

'Oh, love,' I said. 'I wish I could tell you that, I really do. But I can't. No one can. The only thing I can promise you is that, in time, it will get easier to bear. Not go away completely – it'll still be there, of course it will – but it will get easier to cope with, I promise. And in the meantime, if there's anything I can do for you, I will. Would it help if I spoke to your auntie?'

I could hear her sniff. Then she pulled away and wiped the sleeve of her school jumper across her eyes. 'I don't think so, Miss,' she said. 'She's been so lovely, and it's been so hard for her as well. And my cousins are … well …' She shrugged.

'Like all little ones, I expect, sweetheart. Exhausting?'

For which I was rewarded with a wan smile. Perhaps she'd come back to school too soon, I thought. I'd seen that sort of thing before. The bereaved were often buoyed by the attention that surrounds a sudden death, but when lives went back to normal, and the attention began to lessen – that was often when they went down like a ton of bricks. Perhaps what Shona most needed was more opportunity to talk – even just to cry when she needed to, rather than feeling like a visitor, which she must surely do in her aunt's house right now, with the best will in the world. Always on guard. Always polite. Always being on her best behaviour. And she was clearly a good girl. Not the sort to cause trouble. 'You know what I think I should do?' I suggested. 'I think I should speak to the Head and see if we can't up your sessions with your counsellor. What d'you think? It seems to me that what might help would be you being able to be *you* a bit more. To say how you feel without worrying about upsetting anyone. And, of course, I'm always here as well, remember. Always. And you know another trick?'

Shona shook her head. 'No, Miss. I wish I did.'

I gave her another hug and then I winked. 'Punch a cushion. Might not be *quite* as satisfying as bopping Henry,' I added, 'but almost as good – you should give it a try. Now,' I finished, glad to see a bit of colour in her cheeks again. 'How about we launch a raid on those biscuits?'

After the travails of the morning, the afternoon went like a dream. Kelly was free, which was a big help, and also helped me decide on which scenario would be the best one to film. In the end, and ever mindful of the complexity of Unit politics, we settled on Henry's – both because of what had happened between him and Shona, and because his effort was both intelligent and relevant.

Re-casting it solo, he had decided to make Molly the teacher instead, with him as a disruptive pupil – one half of the ongoing argument – little Ben as the teaching assistant and the others as fellow pupils. He'd written the two versions, as I'd asked – one with a bad and one with a good outcome – setting out the opening situation as one in which the teacher was trying to teach the children some chemical symbols, while the disruptive pupil was busy throwing pieces of paper when her back was turned, much to the amusement of the other pupils.

In version one, the TA (played by Ben) called out the disruptive child, and castigated him angrily for behaving like an idiot. This caused the pupil to get angry too, throwing his chair on the floor, and flouncing out of the classroom, which led to even more disruption, and the lesson being interrupted, as the other pupils became disruptive then themselves.

In the second version, however, the TA reacted differently. This time he laughed good-naturedly when the teacher turned round to see what the giggles were about, saying, 'Oh, Miss, it's just Henry doing his magic tricks again. First it's the flying paper trick, as you can see, then it's the one where he magically disappears out of the classroom for a few minutes till you call him back in.'

This caused the other pupils to laugh along with the TA, and made Henry start giggling as well. He then said, 'Sorry, Miss,' to Molly. 'Trust you, Henry,' she chided mildly, accepting his apology. 'Now, if you hold on a few more minutes you can do your other trick as well. The one where you tell me the chemical symbols for the first ten elements!'

'You know what?' Kelly said, putting down Henry's workbook. 'This is brilliant. Not to mention a lesson for me to file away for future use! Seriously, that boy's a proper dark horse, isn't he?'

I nodded. Henry really was a conundrum. Given that his problems relating to his peers were thought to stem from a lack of empathy, he had incredible emotional intelligence. And, as we'd suspected would be the case, the kids really seemed to get the rationale behind the 'good' outcome, all of them chipping in enthusiastically when we played the film back, and getting the point of how you could use humour to change the mood in a classroom, and that resolving conflicts wasn't all about shouting.

Of course, in Imogen's case it wasn't about *any* form of vocalisation, and as the day drew to a close, and I watched Shona and Molly and how they managed her, I wondered what sort of dynamic I'd get to see when I visited her at home. Would the grandparents' conflict-resolution strategies be effective or ineffective? Imogen, too, was a dark horse, and it would be interesting to see.

'Not that I'm expecting to see much conflict, based on what I've seen so far in school,' I said to Kelly. 'I know her grandmother's said she's very vocal at home, but I don't think I'll quite believe it till I actually see it. She's like a ghost, she really is. Completely biddable, does as she's told, obviously takes everything in, but in terms of actually contributing she really is just about invisible.'

'Well, you know what you're always saying about kids who are angels at school ...' Kelly replied.

That they could be devils at home? That they could. Though, somehow, in this case, I doubted it.

The Hinchcliffes lived only a few streets away from the high school, on a road that was in the middle of a post-war estate. It wasn't an area I knew well or had much visited but I had the impression of orderly calm and mostly older residents; there were nets at most of the windows, and cars neatly parked off the road on drives, where I felt sure they'd be religiously washed and polished every Sunday. There was also a distinct lack of children to be seen and the neatly mown verges that sat in front of all the houses looked untroubled by the spectre of flying footballs. Indeed, if there were conflict here I imagined it would be more likely to stem from someone letting their bit of grass grow too long.

I walked up a path flanked by rose bushes, mostly still bearing blooms, underneath which sat huddles of pinky-violet ground plants. And the windows, fairly recently double-glazed, by the look of it, were as nicely dressed as the square of emerald lawn. Which made the commotion I could hear as I raised my hand to use the brass door-knocker feel about as incongruous in this setting as it could be.

It was a male voice I heard first, clear as the best crystal, at almost the same moment when the knocker struck the door. 'I'm warning you,' he raged, 'any more of this and you're out of here. I'm bloody sick of this, you hear me?'

The response came swiftly. 'Get *off* me!' This time the voice was female. 'Get off! I hate you! I fucking *hate* you!'

Wondering quite what to do, since my knock had obviously gone unheeded, I grabbed the knocker and rapped again, only louder. This time the response was so fast it made me jump. I could hear a key being turned in the white PVC door, and it suddenly opened, revealing a rather distressed-looking Mrs Hinchcliffe. She blinked at me, then poked her head out and glanced up and down the empty street, before opening the door just wide enough that I could step inside. 'Come in, Mrs Watson,' she said, beckoning me to get inside quickly. 'Oh, I'm so sorry, really I am, but as you can see …'

And I could see. And what I saw stopped me in my tracks. Because right there, no more than a few feet away from me, was Imogen, still in her school uniform, but with her hair all over the place, and looking more like she belonged to the school of hard knocks than our local comp. She was swinging her arms about wildly, obviously trying to thump her grandfather.

It was with almost a sense of *déjà vu* that I watched Mr Hinchcliffe trying to restrain her, holding on to her wrists and trying to pin her safely against the wall. And the next shock was the realisation that the voice I'd heard before had obviously been Imogen's. 'Get him off me, Nan!' she growled. 'I *mean* it. Get him fucking off me! I want to go to my room! I want to go *to my fucking room*!'

I cleared my throat. 'Mr Hinchcliffe?' I began, trying to make my presence in the hall felt. Imogen could see me but I wasn't sure she was really seeing anything, and as Mr Hinchcliffe had his back to me he definitely couldn't.

At the sound of my voice, though, he turned around and, as if caught red-handed in some illegal act, promptly let his granddaughter go.

'See!' he barked at me. 'See what we have to put up with? All we do for her, and this is how she treats us! You saw that, did you? You've taken a note of that? I bloody hope so, because this is what she's like – every time she can't get her own bloody way!'

Despite her earlier protestations, Imogen seemed in no rush to hot-foot it up to her room now. In fact, she simply sat down on the bottom step of the stairs. So perhaps my presence in the hall had changed her mind, if not her mind-set. She was still busy scowling at her Grandad.

Mrs Hinchcliffe extended a hand and placed it on her husband's forearm nervously. 'Mick, love, let's just all calm down a bit, eh?' she suggested. 'Mrs Watson's from school, remember? Come to see Imogen. Not to stand here and listen to all this stuff.'

I glanced at Imogen then, to find her now staring straight at me with a look of incomprehension on her face. 'That all right with you, love?' I ventured.

There was no answer. Instead she leapt up from where she'd been sitting and made a bolt for the front door, but, rather than open it, she seemed to be grabbing something from it, and by the time I'd realised she wasn't actually trying to get out through it she was already barging past me and sprinting up the stairs.

A door slammed, shaking the air to such an extent that I feared for the grandmother clock on the wall in front of me, which had been quietly marking out time. 'Brilliant,' said Mr Hinchcliffe. 'That's it now. Bloody brilliant!' He rolled his eyes at me, making me think perhaps I'd missed some vital trick, then turned his back and began walking towards the back of the house. 'You weren't in a hurry to be anywhere, were you?' he flung over his shoulder. 'Because you won't be going anywhere for a good bit now, believe me.'

'Oh dear,' said Mrs Hinchcliffe, 'I'm afraid he's right, dear. She's already got the back-door key, you see. Come on,' she said, gesturing that I should follow her husband. 'Come into the kitchen and we'll get the kettle on. Least we can do is make you a cup of tea.'

Completely bewildered, and still a little stunned at having heard Imogen speak finally, I followed Mr Hinchcliffe into a cosy country-style kitchen and, at Mrs Hinchcliffe's invitation, took a seat at the little oilcloth-covered table while she bustled around me with a striped teapot and some teabags.

'Sounds like you're having a bit of an episode,' I ventured.

Mr Hinchcliffe raised his hands and slapped them back palms down on the table. He sat back and looked at me wearily. 'Mrs Watson, you don't know the half of it. Little sod was halfway out of her bedroom window before I managed to drag her back inside again. And threatening to jump again,' he added, glancing in Mrs Hinchcliffe's direction. 'It's getting beyond the pale now. We're having to run the place like bloody Colditz!'

'What?' I said. This was something of an alarming state of affairs. 'Why would she do that?' I asked them both. 'Has she done it before?'

'Why is the sky blue?' her grandmother said, setting down some teacups and saucers. 'And yes, once before. Mick's right. It's getting worse now. The least little thing and it's always the same. She's going to jump out of the window and break her legs. She's going to run in front of a bus. She's going to throw herself on a railway line. And so on and so forth. And then we'll be sorry, apparently.' She sighed heavily, and I felt for her. She looked exhausted. 'And that's the problem, Mrs Watson. We have no idea what sets her off. Almost anything, it seems,' she added, casting her eyes towards the ceiling. 'Just lashes out at us, doesn't she, Mick? So it's no wonder, really, is it?' She glanced at her husband again and shook her head. 'Oh, I know what you're thinking,' she said to me. 'I know how it's been. She's silent as a thief in the night when she's in school, isn't she? Bottles it up, see. Keeps her nose clean. Wouldn't say boo to a goose. And then *we're* the ones who get it,' she said, adding a milk jug to the pile of crockery. 'We're the ones that have to bloody pay for it as soon as she gets home!'

I nodded sympathetically. 'I do understand,' I said. 'And Imogen's not unusual in that respect. Children need to let off steam, and it's usually the place where they feel most secure where they feel the –'

'Let off steam!' Mr Hinchcliffe huffed. 'She's like Stephenson's bloody *Rocket*! We're at our wits' end with her, Mrs Watson. And we're too old for all this nonsense! I mean it's one thing stepping in to help out and give our son a break – never minded doing that – but it's been almost three bloody months and we've had enough of it! I'm on the list for a knee op and what'll happen once I get my bloody date? That's what I want to know!'

'I know,' I said, anxious to steer the conversation back to Imogen and what had been the root of what was beginning to sound like an increasingly volatile situation. 'It must feel like a huge burden on you both. Which is why we're so keen to do what we can as a school to help get to the root of Imogen's problems. We have a specialist coming into school on Monday, in fact, to tell us a little more about her selective mutism …' I could see I was losing Mr Hinchcliffe at this point, as he was shaking his head in a pretty resigned way. 'And how about your son?' I suggested, changing tack. 'Have you spoken to him about how difficult you're finding things?'

The Hinchcliffes exchanged another glance and I sensed a difference of opinion was simmering just below the surface. 'I don't think there's much he can do,' Mrs Hinchcliffe said eventually. 'It's complicated, Mrs Watson,' she added. 'They're not really speaking at the moment.'

'Ah,' I said, wondering if she'd offer any more by way of explanation. But she didn't, and I wondered if this was a current bone of contention – that they wanted Imogen to go home to her father and he wasn't playing ball. But I decided to leave it. For now the key thing was to get Imogen opening up. Only once she did so would I have any idea how *she* felt, which might be completely at odds with the line I was being peddled. Kids acted out because they were hurting, and very often because their voices weren't being heard, or because the adults caring for them were putting their own needs first. This was a complex family dynamic, and, however saintly the new girlfriend who had launched into the fray, a teenager who'd been abandoned by her mother was a distressed teenager in most cases, and distressed teenagers could be volatile, antagonistic and aggressive, as the Hinchcliffes were undoubtedly learning.

'So,' I said, 'back in the here and now, what's the business with the key all about?'

Mrs Hinchcliffe poured boiling water into the teapot. 'Like Mick says, we live like prisoners in our own home at the moment.'

'But why does she take the keys? It's not as if you lock her up, is it? I mean, she walks to school and back on her own every day …'

'Oh, it's not because she's going to run away,' Mr Hinchcliffe said. 'She just does it to be bloody-minded! We lock the upstairs windows, so she takes the downstairs keys.'

'An issue with control, then …' I mused.

'Is that what they're calling it these days?' Mr Hinchcliffe said, stirring the tea. 'An issue with needing a clip round the ear, if you ask me!'

Mrs Hinchcliffe placed cups on saucers and as she did so I could see her fingers were shaking. They were small hands, dainty and delicate, almost translucent in places. I looked up to smile at her and was shocked to see tears brimming in her eyes.

There was a slight quiver around her chin, too, but I got a strong sense that I should pretend I hadn't seen either.

'Well, as I say,' I said briskly, turning my attention to Mr Hinchcliffe, 'we have a specialist coming into school on Monday, and –'

'Bloody doctors,' Mr Hinchcliffe said. 'They're bloody simple, they are, those head doctors. Her last school sent her to one of them and where did that get us? Nowhere. No, she doesn't need a doctor. She just needs to bloody toughen up! Not put all this stress on her nan just to get her own way. It's wicked, that's what it is. It's wicked. If she wants to start on anyone she should start on the horrible little gits doing the name-calling! Not her bloody grandmother – look at the state of her!'

Mrs Hinchcliffe bit her lip and looked daggers at her husband. 'Well, whatever the whys and wherefores,' I said, realising that we could go on like this till midnight, 'how about if I go up and see if I can persuade Imogen to talk to me. Would that be okay? And maybe coax her down, too. Then we can all have that cuppa.'

Mrs Hinchcliffe had now pulled a hankie from her cardigan sleeve and blew into it delicately while her husband poured the tea. 'You can try,' she said. 'No harm in trying. Though what good it'll do I don't know.'

'Well, if not actually talk to me, at *least* listen to me,' I said. 'And if nothing else, I need to be able to get home at some point, don't I? Or do you have the fire brigade on speed dial?'

It took a second or two for Mr Hinchcliffe to get the joke.

# Chapter 8

'You were locked in their *house*?' Mike spluttered, as I tried to explain where I'd got to. I'd called him too, but as my phone battery was almost dead to the world, it had been to tell him little more than that I was on my way. I pulled off my jacket and dumped my bag in the hall. 'But that's ridiculous!' he huffed. 'What were the school thinking of, sending you there in the first place?'

I couldn't help but smile. Yes, it was almost seven, and I was normally home by five, but it was hardly the wee hours and this was hardly a huge drama. It was the home of a couple of pensioners and a slight teenage girl – hardly *The Texas Chainsaw Massacre* or *The Silence of the Lambs*.

I found myself smiling ruefully as I followed Mike through into the kitchen. Actually, on the silence front, there *was* a parallel.

I'd gone upstairs, past a row of horticultural prints of various roses, to find myself on a small landing, crowded with small bits of dark wood furniture – a spindly chair; a semi-circular side table, topped with a vase of silk roses, themselves sitting on a small embroidered doilie; a wooden wall-mounted repository for a large thimble collection; and, over the banister rail, a pair of beige towels. Dust, I thought. A dust haven. It made me anxious just to look at it. When I was retired, I decided, I would have to live an ornament-free existence, just to stay on the right side of sane.

The little landing was also crowded by some very busy floral wallpaper and punctuated by an assortment of panelled white doors. Following the instructions Mrs Hinchcliffe had given me, I knocked on the one to the left of the bathroom and, getting no response, turned the handle and went in.

It was exactly as I'd expected, given the rest of the Hinchcliffes' home. Prettily decorated and furnished, creamy floral curtains, a selection of cheerful pictures, sunny aspect … In fact, the perfect cosy guest bedroom, should that be what you were after. And, just as had been the case when I'd first seen Imogen's clothes, nothing like a teenage girl's bedroom at all. I winced to see there wasn't so much as a duvet, let alone a funky duvet cover, much less any trace of the usual detritus such as hair straighteners, nail varnish bottles, discarded socks and bras.

Imogen herself was sitting on the single bed, atop a quilted floral bedspread, head down, nose in a paperback book. She looked up, and, seeing me, her face took on that same closed expression that I had by now become so familiar with in school.

'Hello,' I said, to which she responded by putting the book down, uncrossing her legs and swinging them around and to the floor. She didn't stand up, though, so I went and sat beside her.

'Can we talk,' I asked her gently, 'about what's troubling you?'

I left it long enough to feel fairly sure she'd decided she didn't want to communicate, then picked up the book to see what it was. It was from the school library, a book by Jacqueline Wilson, called *Double Act*, which I recognised immediately as being one of the set texts some of the year 8s were currently reading.

'I don't think I've read this one,' I said, scanning the blurb on the back and flicking through a couple of pages. It seemed to be about twin sisters, Ruby and Garnet, whose mum had died – so a parallel with Imogen's life right there. 'It looks good,' I said. 'Are you enjoying it? I love Jacqueline Wilson's books, don't you? I think my daughter's read almost every one she's ever written.'

Again, there was no response, so I put it down again, changing tack. 'Well,' I said, 'that was certainly some introduction to your voice, anyway, Imogen. I was so surprised I nearly lost mine, you know that? But I understand that perhaps you don't want to talk to me today. I just came up to let you know that, well, that I've had a chat with your nan and grandad, and the one thing you need to know is that we're all in this together. Imogen, sweetie, we all want to *help* you. That and the small matter,' I continued, 'that if I don't get the front-door key I'm not going to get home,

I won't get any tea and, more importantly, I am going to miss *EastEnders*.'

I was close enough to nudge her so I took a risk and did. 'So can we resolve this particular conflict, do you think?'

'So she gave it to you?' asked Mike, when I'd finished relating everything to him. 'Just like that?'

'Just like that,' I said, surveying the plate he placed in front of me and sniffing. 'And don't worry, no fishy business whatsoever.'

Riley wafted into the living room, just as Mike was groaning at my lame joke. 'Those fish fingers are gross, Mum. Just gross. God – and look at them! Dad, you've cremated them!'

I was inclined to agree, bless him, but said nothing. I'd just kind of work my way around to them, via the mash and mushy peas.

'But it's still not on,' Mike said. 'Yes, it might have been okay on this occasion, but I'm not sure this business of you making home visits isn't a bit above and beyond the call of duty.'

'Love, it was my choice,' I said. 'They don't make me do anything. But it's part of my job to work with and support parents. And indeed grandparents. So I *want* to. Anyway, I'm glad I went. I feel I've learned so much more about everything now.'

Which wasn't strictly true – what the visit had mostly done was throw up more questions. But that was fine. It at least gave me something to work with. And I'd been particularly pleased that Imogen had so meekly given me the key as soon as I'd requested it. She clearly had a respect for authority, and, hopefully, me – and I knew that would help a great deal.

'Even so,' Mike persisted, 'I still think it's a bit much for an unaccompanied female to be visiting strangers' homes in the evening. I know you see it as part of your job, all this "super-nanny" stuff, but it's still risky, and at the very least you should keep your phone switched on, love – I must have tried you a dozen times. I didn't know what to think!'

I felt a bit bad about that. I wasn't the best person to be left in charge of a mobile phone and I knew it. I was forever leaving it switched on in school and having it burst into song in meetings, or forgetting I'd switched it off and running around for hours after school was over, oblivious to the fact that people might be trying to get in touch with me, and, as for remembering to charge it at night, I was a lost cause.

Riley laughed. 'Didn't know how to cook fish fingers, more like,' she trilled, then skipped off into the hall with an 'Out with David, home by ten!', narrowly avoiding a flick across the back of the knees with Mike's tea-towel.

'That was absolutely delicious, love,' I lied as I gave him the plate back. 'So, Kieron, how was your second day?'

My own day was still some distance from being over, which was pretty much par for the course now. It hadn't always been so; when I'd started in my job I had several free periods allocated during the school day, in order that I could keep on top of the paperwork. But with the increasing numbers of children who were sent to the Unit, that particular luxury was beginning to become a thing of the past. I didn't mind, though. Were I a mainstream teacher I'd be doing a lot of that sort of thing anyway, and though it sometimes meant I was exhausted come Friday, it was all an important part of the learning curve.

It turned out that Kieron's second day had mostly been 'epic' so, though he'd been chewing on his fingers – a sure sign that he was stressed about something – I reassured myself that it was probably a productive kind of stress. So once he'd filled me in on how he and Si were already composing some music for a presentation, I was able to turn my attention back to work.

An important part of my job involved writing up detailed reports on every child that I currently had on my books. These would be passed on to the learning support department, the appropriate head of year and, if applicable, to Gary, our Child Protection Officer, and form part of the dossier of information we had on every pupil who needed extra support.

In Imogen's case, an important addition to what we already knew would be the details of my home visit earlier. Though there was still a great deal we didn't know – and probably needed to, if we were to have the tools to help her – I'd at least gained more insight into what was clearly a tense and difficult family dynamic.

I wondered too, as I wrote, how things might have changed. One thing I'd learned since starting my job was that, following a home visit, the dynamic between me and the child usually shifted. And in a positive way, too; it tended to become more personal. There was something

Casey Watson

about seeing a child away from the school setting – with all those rules and protocols – that encouraged a greater rapport.

That said, we were talking about a child who'd yet to speak to me, so I wasn't holding my breath that we'd suddenly become confidantes. So it was to my delight that I arrived at my classroom door the following morning to find Imogen standing there waiting for me to arrive.

'Hello love,' I said, fumbling with my key in the lock, aware of just how early it still was. 'That's good timing. Could you grab my satchel off my shoulder for me so I can get the door open, do you think? This stupid lock needs some WD40.'

If she was aware of the irony of my words she didn't show it. She did, however, take the bag off my shoulder so that I could maintain a hold on the stack of books I was carrying in one hand while jiggling the key in the class-room door in the other.

Once we were in she went straight across to my desk and placed the satchel down carefully upon it. She then walked over to the evidence boards on the classroom wall and, while I filled the kettle and popped it on its stand, stood and studied all the new pieces of work I'd put up the previous afternoon. One of the things I'd copied and added was Henry's conflict-resolution play synopsis, which she seemed to be studying quite intently.

'It's good, isn't it?' I called across. 'There's a lot more to Henry than meets the eye, as you've probably already noticed!'

She nodded, and even glanced over and smiled at this. It

94

was still as odd, though – as odd as it had ever been – being in a classroom alone with a person who didn't speak. I wondered about actors who had to do action scenes in front of green screens; how they managed to fight digitally produced monsters they could only imagine rather than see. It was strange talking into a void; it felt like such an unnatural thing to be doing: And it occurred to me that it must be even stranger for Imogen – hearing words spoken but not being able to respond to them. Was she trying to, I wondered? I couldn't quite imagine what it must be like. It was clearly psychological but, to her, did it feel physical? As if she was desperate to get something out but couldn't make her body obey her brain?

Or was it not like that? Was it more of a decision she had to stick to? Like my endless quests to give up smoking, was it something she *did* have physical control over, and had to will herself not to crack and open her mouth?

It was while I was pondering this that I noticed that, while she was looking at something else, Imogen's lips were moving, presumably in synch with what she was reading – something I'd not noticed before. She then walked across to the girls' table with her workbook and began reading that – and, once again, she seemed to be miming what she saw.

Or was she? 'What was that, love?' I said casually, while spooning coffee into my mug. 'I couldn't quite hear what you said. Say again?'

'I thought she …' she began, but I couldn't quite catch the rest of it because the kettle was chuntering up to the boil.

I flipped the switch up. 'Sorry, love?' I said.

'I thought she might …' she whispered. At least I *thought* that was what she'd whispered. I came round to the front of my desk. 'You thought someone might *what*?' I repeated. But as soon as I began to approach her it was as if her own switch had been flipped as well. It was as if a shutter had come down, the change was so abrupt and so decisive. As if she'd mentally run from me, to a far corner of her mind.

I decided I wouldn't push it. I would simply ponder it, for the moment at least. Make a note after I'd made my coffee and then mull over what it might mean. It was a breakthrough – a *big* breakthrough – and that was a good enough start for me. And with the arrival of Gavin, seconds later, full of his usual surfeit of energy, I switched mental gears – *I must really chase up the parents re that medication*, I registered.

*New hat on, Casey*, I thought, as the rest tumbled in behind him. *Let the day's madness begin …*

# Chapter 9

It was clear as I got ready for work the following Monday morning that winter was very much on its way. We were now well into October and not only were the mornings getting darker, but the temperature had taken a nose-dive as well. I made a mental note to ask Mike to reset the timer on the heating and hot water as I shivered in the bedroom after my necessarily brief shower; brief because of the lack of hot water, rather than because I was in a hurry. With the meeting with the clinician scheduled, I had the rare luxury of time, as my fellow behaviour manager, Jim Dawson, would be taking the class for the morning in my place.

Though we shared a job title, our roles were very different. Neither of us knew it at the time, but there had originally been just the one post up for grabs, so we'd actually started out as competitors. But after we'd both given presentations on how best we thought behaviour could be improved and emotional literacy fostered, it seemed the school had something of a rethink. Seeing so much merit in incorporating our different ideas and approaches, they'd decided to create two jobs and, though it would stretch the budget, employ both of us and let us divide the role as the pair of us saw fit. They also put at our disposal the services the school's TAs and learning support staff.

So that's what we'd done, divvying thing up according to our own 'skill-sets' (to use the jargon) so that I ran the Unit, while Jim's role was more peripatetic: he could often be found pounding the mean streets of the school corridors, chasing after some errant or absconding child or other. In the main, though, he was classroom-based, drafted in as and where needed. If a teacher was having problems with a particularly disruptive pupil, Jim was the go-to guy to form a cunning plan to contain the chaos.

This morning, however, Jim was going to contain any chaos that might break out with my little lot, ably assisted by Kelly. All I needed to do was set things up for that morning's activities, and though I knew that there wasn't *that* much need for me to organise every tiny detail, I was far too much the control freak not to do so.

And it seemed I wasn't the only one keen to get a march on the day. As I walked in through the reception doors the first people I clapped eyes on were Henry and little Ben sitting quietly on two of the black seating cubes that were normally reserved for visitors and parents.

'Good morning, boys,' I said, eyeing them curiously. 'Now, it's far too early in the day for you both to be in trouble. So, let me see, are you waiting for me?'

They both jumped up and Henry grinned at me.

'Yes, we were,' he said, 'weren't we, Ben?'

Ben nodded. 'Just so you know we'll keep an eye on things for you. You know, till you get back after dinner … you will be back after dinner, Miss, won't you?'

I was quite sure that was the most Ben had so far said to me in one go, without prompting. Which was very pleasing. I'd not personally found him that challenging so far but he was a boy whose reputation for causing trouble among his peers definitely preceded him.

I was also pleased that these two were clearly forming some sort of bond, and I made a mental note to check if they shared a route to school, since this wasn't the first time they seemed to have arrived in school together.

'Yes, I will,' I told him. 'And thank you so much for reassuring me. It always helps to know there will be a few people who'll help things run smoothly.'

'And we'll keep an eye on Imogen for you, Miss,' Henry added. 'And I won't get into nothing with Shona, neither. Just in case you were wondering, that's all.'

'Well, that's good to know as well, Henry,' I said, trying to suppress a laugh as I ruffled the hair of first the taller and then the shorter of the boys' heads. 'I can go off to my meeting without worrying now, can't I? Thank you both.' I glanced at the big clock on the wall. 'But, if I'm not mistaken, the bell is going to go at any minute, so if the two of you are going to be my undercover helpers you'd better scoot off. You won't be able to help me if Mr Dawson sends you out for being late, will you?'

They scooted off and I headed off to the staffroom for a coffee. I had 20 minutes to spare and I intended to make the most of them. The staffroom was heaving, as it always was at that time of the morning: everyone dashing around, collecting internal mail from their pigeon holes, grabbing paperwork, scribbling last-minute notes, marking last-minute books – all of them trying to cram a quart's worth of organising into a pint-pot, before the ringing of the dreaded bell. It didn't seem to matter how passionate any of us felt about our jobs – when your day was dictated by the tyranny of that buzzer, your response was exactly like that of one of Pavlov's dogs; it meant 'Showtime – you'd better be ready!'

The room cleared as if by magic moments later, leaving me with a steaming mug of instant and an upbeat frame of mind. It was the little things that brought on that happy mindset, and this was one such – the simple matter of Henry and Ben's thoughtfulness was enough to lift my day.

Despite their well-documented penchant for disruption and violent outbursts, I had a soft spot for both of these boys. Which was probably part of my job spec – being keen to unearth the positive in a difficult child was pretty much essential – but it was still pleasing to be feeling it, rather than just doing it.

Both boys lived chaotic lives and both had huge self-esteem issues, and I was particularly pleased to see Ben, who I was only just getting to know, showing potential for having more productive relationships with his peers.

I tried to imagine what it must be like to be him. According to his notes, it was his birth that had precipitated his mother's death. She'd been a non-attender at her antenatal clinics and had suffered from undiagnosed pre-eclampsia, which, tragically, was caught too late and resulted in her death. This left her newborn child to be taken home by his shocked and grieving father – the only child of a man who hadn't the first clue how to raise one.

But with no other family in the area, it seemed Ben's dad lacked either a choice in the matter or much support and, from what Gary Clark had told me, had taken to drinking too, in recent years, and when drunk would regularly point out to his frightened, bewildered son that if it hadn't been for him his mother would still be alive.

What a burden for a child to carry. No wonder poor Ben was angry all the time.

It was Imogen who was bubbling to the surface of my mind again as I walked the short distance between the staff-room and Gary's office. Imogen had actually started to say something to me on Friday, something my instinct told me might be important. I was therefore itching to see what the specialist had to say and what kind of strategies he might be able to suggest to help me coax her to say something more.

Mr Gregory was an experienced speech and language therapist with a special interest in selective mutism, and I was pleased to see he didn't look too scary. It was silly, and I always berated myself for it, but without a string of letters after my name I had always felt a little intimidated when faced with suited and booted professionals. I was confident in my abilities, I worked hard, and knew I was good enough to justify my position – I just couldn't get past the feeling that I didn't have the credentials to prove it, I supposed. Not a chip on the shoulder – I had nothing but respect for my colleagues; just that nagging voice – that women in particular are so good at – that I was lucky to count myself as one of their number, despite Mike endlessly telling me not to be so daft.

But there was nothing to fear here, and I felt immediately at ease. He was a genial man in what I guessed was his early sixties, and straight away I realised the meeting wouldn't be as formal as I'd thought.

'You can put those away,' he said, chuckling, seeing me and Gary both arming ourselves with pens and notebooks. 'I haven't come here to deliver a lecture; just to chat about what we already know about the girl and see if I can suggest some techniques you could try in order to get her to start talking again. Of course,' he added, 'whether that happens – not to mention when – will depend to a great extent on what made her choose silence in the first place.'

'So that is a fact, then,' I asked, 'that the child actively chooses not to talk?'

Mr Gregory made a yes and no gesture with his hands. 'It's probably too simplistic to talk in those terms, but, to an extent, yes – in that it's an anxiety disorder rather than a physical one, whether it's conscious or not. It's usually something that happens to a child who already has a nervous disposition, and that in itself is often inherited from a parent.'

*Which parent in this case?* I found myself wondering. Mum or dad? That in itself would be a useful thing to know.

'Children with SM,' Mr Gregory went on, 'are characterised by their ability to speak normally in an environment in which they're comfortable – say, at home – but unable to communicate in stressful social situations, of which school, for most children, is the most obvious example.

'It often starts young, too – typically when a child first encounters school or nursery, and it needs careful, consistent management if it's not to become a self-fulfilling prophecy. It's one of those mental health disorders, sadly, that feeds off itself, so the last thing to do is to leave it to sort itself out in the hopes that it will get better, because generally it won't.

'There is another type of SM, however, that can be brought on by a specific stressful life-event or sudden trauma. This is slightly different in that it tends to be more conscious a withdrawal of speech; they are choosing not to speak as a way of retreating from the reality of an unbearable situation. Again, if this is left unchecked, the prognosis tends to be poor, as it can then morph into the former type of SM, with all the negative ramifications that has.'

Mr Gregory paused for breath, then smiled. 'Does that all make sense?'

Gary nodded, and I resisted the urge to reach again for my notebook. I was itching to write all this down. 'Yes, it does,' Gary said. 'And I suppose the first thing we need to do is identify exactly where Imogen fits into this. She's obviously not been mute since pre-school – well, as far as her records show, anyway – and from what we've heard from her grandparents' – he glanced across at me – 'she's the antithesis of the shy, nervous type at home.'

I nodded. 'And I've seen that for myself, when I visited. From what I've seen, Imogen isn't an anxious child, particularly – just a challenging and deeply unhappy one.'

'So you heard her speak, then?' Mr Gregory asked.

'Yes and no. I *heard* her shouting, but I didn't actually see her. Her grandparents told me she always was very vocal – and extremely demanding, too – but as soon as she was aware of my presence she stopped speaking immediately.'

'I think you've probably just answered Mr Clark's question, then,' Mr Gregory said. 'And having looked at the notes you emailed, the picture seems reasonably clear. Imogen's selective mutism is probably a post-traumatic coping mechanism. In which case the key thing is to find out what's caused it. Which is the poser, of course – since, unless we find a way in, she's not going to tell you.'

'She did try to speak to me, actually,' I said. 'At least I think she did. Last Friday.'

I told them both about the few words Imogen had managed to get out, and how I'd been pondering what they might mean all weekend.

'The mother, perhaps?' Gary wondered. 'It would be interesting to find out more about that whole situation, wouldn't it? What actually happened there. How rare must it be for a mother to leave her child so completely?'

'And so suddenly, come to that,' I agreed.

'It certainly sounds as if the mother leaving might be the root,' Mr Gregory said. 'Though this happened a couple of years back, did it not?' We both nodded. 'Yet the SM is fairly recent – a matter of months, isn't it? What about the grandmother? How do you think things are there?'

'Difficult to tell,' I said. 'Though I know both grandparents are at the end of their tether. As I suppose they would be, given their age and state of health. And there's also the step-mum, of course – she was apparently also at her wits' end; in fact, it's the step-mum who appears to have been the main target of Imogen's distress. That's why the grandparents have her living with them now – because she simply couldn't cope with Imogen's tantrums any more.'

'Of course, what we most need,' Gary said, 'is for Imogen herself to *tell* us what's wrong, isn't it?'

I nodded. 'Which is only going to happen if we can get her to speak while she's in school. Which is the problem. Because as soon as she was aware she had my full attention when she did speak, it was like a physical shut-down. Wham! Shop closed till further notice, you know?'

'Well,' said Mr Gregory, 'that's mostly what I'm here for. To give you a selection of strategies to try, in order to bring that happy state of affairs about. So, to start …'

Now I did open my notebook.

An hour and a half and four mugs of coffee later Gary and I were armed with what almost felt like an information overload – it seems there were as many ways of trying to crack the code of a child's selective mutism as there were reason for them 'choosing silence' in the first place. I learned something else, too – that a lot of the strategies I'd been reading about on the internet, and which I'd thought sounded logical, were, in fact, absolute no-nos. I grinned to myself as I headed back to the staffroom, thinking how I might not run that particular one past Mike. Being non-digital-age compliant almost as a career choice, my husband was always sceptical about my internet browsing and the 'facts' it threw up. 'The internet isn't God, Casey,' he'd often be heard pontificating from on high. 'Just because bloody googly, or whatever it is, says so, that doesn't automatically make it right!'

But it was with that in mind that I took advantage of the hour I had to kill before the lunch bell; which I spent in a quiet corner of the staffroom, with both computer *and* books, to try and pull together – or at least make a start on pulling together – some sort of reference guide of strategies we could put in place for Imogen right away.

I thought she might *what*? That was the first question I wanted to answer. Might come home again? Might send me back to Dad's? Might have abandoned me? Answer that, instinct told me, and we'd be on our way.

# Chapter 10

I was buzzing by the time I got home from work that evening. I felt all the new stuff I'd learned whooshing round in my head, and on the verge of a very important breakthrough. I knew that all I had to do was to work out and apply the right strategy, and bingo. What that was going to be exactly, I hadn't quite worked out yet, but I was determined to keep up the momentum.

'So, after tea,' I told Mike as he washed his hands at the kitchen sink, 'I'm going to set up shop at the dining table and finish writing up my plans – I know I can do it.'

'Do what?'

'Get Imogen to speak, of course. Haven't you been listening to what I've been saying?'

He had not long got home from work and he looked tired – he'd had an early start. I huffed even so, but he didn't rise to it.

'Case, love,' he said, 'you know what your "strategy" should be? Give her a dose of whatever it is you've got. Not too much, mind,' he added, moving prudently out of punching range. 'Or the poor kid won't know when to shut up!'

Kieron, who was sitting in the lounge, 'apparently' watching telly, hooted with laughter. 'Nice one, Dad,' he called.

'Nice one, my foot!' I said. 'This is important!'

'Love, I *know* it is,' Mike said more seriously. 'And I'm happy that you've had a good day. But all this bringing your work home malarkey – I thought you said you were going to try not to do it? Not quite so much, at any rate. What about just sitting down and watching *EastEnders* for a change? You know, like we used to. In the olden days.'

'Yeah, Mum,' Kieron chipped in. 'What about us? We'll be neglected children soon. Officially.'

'Oh, give over,' I told them. 'And you're hardly children any more. And it's not like I'm doing it all the time, is it? It's just that this is a complicated case and I really want to crack it.'

Riley, also home from work and dishing up stew and dumplings from the slow cooker, snorted in a derogatory fashion. 'Case to crack! Mum, who d'you think you are – Columbo? Honestly!'

Suitably chastised, I accepted my bowl of stew and began to eat it. It tasted surprisingly like humble pie. I knew they were mostly just ribbing me but perhaps I was taking my job just a little bit too seriously. Or maybe I wasn't – maybe taking it seriously was what was needed, but perhaps I should try to shut up a bit more about it once I was home. I watched Kieron and Riley laughing with their dad about something they'd all been watching last night on the telly with mixed feelings. I'd been doing paperwork, and perhaps I should have taken a break from it, but, actually, parts of my job *were* quite serious. And none of it would get done by itself. So perhaps I just needed to manage my time better. Stay a little later after school, perhaps, so that once I did get home finally, I *could* sit down with them all and watch *EastEnders*.

Which, once tea was out of the way, I duly did.

I did manage to sneak an hour in later, however, so when I got to school the following morning I was raring to go – I just hoped there would be less in the way of soap-opera style drama when I got there. The big thing that I'd learned, amid all the medical terminology and jargon, was that I had actually been going about things all wrong, and actually unwittingly reinforcing Imogen's refusal – or, more accurately – her perceived inability to speak. By allowing her to retreat and not encouraging her to interact better with her peers and with myself, I had given her the green light to remain silent.

It had seemed logical to me, of course. I was used to using a softly-softly approach with a child who was trauma-tised and self-conscious; giving them time to get used to their new environment and settle themselves into it a little before expecting them to come out of their shells. According to Mr Gregory, however, this wasn't helping at all. I needed to use behavioural therapy techniques to show Imogen that remaining silent wasn't an option – well, not for that much longer, anyway. Her silence wasn't to be rewarded – that would just reinforce the behaviour; instead I must lavish praise at any and all attempts at communication; this would help retrain her unconscious mind so that speaking stopped being a source of fear.

First off, I took a couple of days to orient myself, watching her various strategies for responding to attempts to communicate with her, both by myself and by the others in the group. With her fellow pupils, it tended to be a case of ignoring her – which was isolating, obviously – or over-compensating, allowing her to get away with not speaking, much as an older sibling often did with a younger child.

With me, it was a case of mostly winging it. If I drew attention to her in class, she would habitually hang her head and look downwards, with the sort of 'If I can't see you, you can't see me' logic a much younger child would use. She'd blush as well – perhaps part of the reason why it worked, because, anxious not to further stress an already stressed and bullied child, I would 'let her off' by moving swiftly on.

But now it was time for some tough love. Not an abrupt about-turn – that really would stress her too much, I judged – just a slow shift towards a more robust strategy. Now, if I called her name in class, I kept the spotlight firmly on her for as long as it took to get some sort of reaction, even if it wasn't speech itself. It could be a nod or a head shake, an action, such as getting something for me, or passing something to someone else. The main thing was to make her a more dynamic part of the group, so she couldn't retreat into herself.

And by the Thursday I was already seeing progress. So

much so that by the time Friday morning came around I thought I'd try something more radical that I'd read about.

We were doing work on emotions; something that cropped up in the unit often, for obvious reasons. I'd had the children cut out a giant paper firework the previous afternoon, which we were going to use in the exercise this morning. It would be Firework Night before long, after all. That said, this was more about empathy than Guy Fawkes. Unlike the hapless gunpowder plotter, empathy was a perennial.

'Right,' I told the children, having pinned up the rocket and grabbed a pen, 'what I want you to do is tell me words that describe negative emotions, okay? I'll call out names and I want you to shout out a word, then I'll write them all on this magnificent rocket, ready for us to whoosh off into space. Got that?'

Heads nodded.

'Yeah,' said Ben. 'But what about the tree?'

I'd also had the children cut out and paint a big tree, plus a pile of apples, all ready to be written on as well. 'We're going to do that next, Ben,' I explained. 'Once we've got rid of all the negative feelings we're going to accentuate the positive. And "accentuate" means what? Does anybody know?'

'Make more of it, Miss,' Shona supplied quietly.

'Exactly, Shona,' I said, turning round to face the rocket. This part – facing away from them – was key. 'Right, then,' I said, pen poised, 'um … let me see … Ben. You can start. Let's have a word, please.'

'Um, angry, Miss?' he suggested.

'Very good, Ben,' I said. 'That's a great word to send off to space.' I then wrote it down, and remained facing the wall. 'So … Shona. You can be next. A word, please?'

'Lonely, Miss,' Shona supplied.

I wrote that one down too. 'Henry, next. Can you come up with a word for me, Henry?'

'I was going to say angry, Miss, but Ben already pinched it.'

'I didn't *pinch* it. I just thought of it!'

'Yeah, well, fighting, then, Miss,' he sniffed. 'My word's going to be fighting.'

I resisted the urge to turn back round and check that they weren't actually doing any. 'You're on the right lines, Henry,' I said, 'but it needs to be a word that describes how you might feel. Not so much *do*, as *feel*, you know? Can you think of one like that?'

'How about scared, Miss?' he said eventually.

'Scared is excellent, Henry. Thank you.' I added it to the rocket. 'Okay, so now it's … let me see. Imogen. Yes, Imogen. What's your word going to be?'

I remained with my pen poised just below Henry's 'scared', knowing that all eyes, bar mine, would be on Imogen. The silence lengthened, but I stayed where I was.

'D'you mean me, Miss?' asked Molly eventually. 'You haven't had my word yet. My word's upset. I'd already thinked it.'

'No, sweetie,' I said, pretending to go over the lines of the words already up there. I felt sure they were all bewildered by my refusal to turn around. 'That's a great word, and we'll definitely use it, but Imogen was next on my list. Imogen, have you thought of one?'

Again, the silence was deafening. And I came within a whisker of turning round and moving on, when, in the tiniest voice imaginable – a voice that was nothing like the one I'd heard through the front door of her grandparents' house – I clearly heard the word 'sad'.

'What was that, Imogen?' I said quickly, hoping against hope that it had been her, and not just one of the lads, mucking around. But the silence told me it *was* her who'd spoken.

'Sad,' she said again, ever so slightly more loudly. 'Sad,' I repeated. 'Excellent word, Imogen. Well done.'

I quickly added it and now I did turn around finally. Imogen looked fraught – I could think of no other word to describe it – and as if she might at any time burst into tears. Molly, sitting next to her, was staring at her, open-mouthed, and the other children were looking at each other, all obviously astonished. I would now have to quickly get them back on track before the attention on Imogen became completely unbearable.

'Right,' I said. 'Molly. Remind me what your word was again?'

'Upset, Miss,' she said, turning to Imogen. 'Which is a bit like your word, isn't it? Isn't it, Miss?'

I agreed that indeed it was. Similar but slightly different. 'Now, Gavin,' I said. 'My little whizz-kid – what's your word?'

If the tension hadn't quite diffused, I knew it soon would. Gavin would, I was sure, come up with something kooky.

And he obliged. 'Badalicious!' he said, adding a fist-pump for good measure, and having the rest of them collapse into giggles.

'I'll take the first bit of that, Gavin,' I said, adding a smile of my own. 'As I'm not quite sure "badalicious" has yet made it into the dictionary. No doubt it will eventually, but for now bad will do perfectly. Which means that, now, we can move on to our apples. Though in this case,' I added, feeling very jaunty about my little breakthrough, 'I hope there won't be any "bad" apples.'

Of course, I then had to explain what a 'bad apple' was, but, all in all, a good half-morning's work.

'It was just incredible!' I enthused to Kelly and Gary that lunchtime. 'I couldn't believe it. I mean, I know the whole point of getting an expert in and devising strategies and so on is because they do work, but, still. It went like clock-work. I couldn't believe it,' I said again. 'And then she did it again – when we were doing the apples – she came out with "love".'

Kelly was nodding vigorously, clearly as excited as I was, though Gary – longer in the tooth and less inclined to hyperbole – merely grinned. 'Well, that was definitely one of the items on the to-do list,' he agreed. 'One you can now tick off. Good work, Casey. Let's hope it now continues. I'll let the other key staff know as well, as this probably needs to be a concerted effort. Do you think it's worth calling the grandparents, too – let them know we've made some progress?'

I shook my head, and mentally reined myself in. It was

exciting, yes, but in the big scheme of things not *that* exciting. Two words did not a conversation make, after all.

'No,' I said, finally. 'I'd rather we hung on a little longer. I'm sure there's more to come, and when it does we'll have a chance of getting to the bottom of it, won't we? And if we say anything now, and they bring it up, it just might put her back, mightn't it? Might make her feel she's being hounded into speaking. No, if you don't mind, I'd like to press on a bit more first. Try some of the other fiendishly clever tricks I have up my sleeve ...'

Which, of course, I did, the following one being stimulus withdrawal, which I was keen to put into practice the following week. This, I explained to Gary and Kelly, was designed to give the child a second safe alternative, the idea being that once they'd got used to speaking to a certain person, in a certain environment, you introduced another person into that successful situation – not with a view to forcing the child to speak to them, but rather as a constant unthreatening presence. You then had to engineer a situation where it was almost impossible for the child to avoid speaking, even though the other person was there.

'Isn't that what happened this morning?' Kelly wanted to know. 'I mean, the rest of the class were there, weren't they?'

'Yes and no,' I said. 'Yes, they were there, but speaking in front of them really stressed Imogen. The idea of this is that she can speak to me when they're there, and *without* being stressed, which is where making it more of a "two-on-one" scenario comes in.'

Kelly's brows knitted. 'Sounds very technical.'

'I know,' I said, 'but it's all in my notes, so don't worry. The important thing is that now that we've finally got the ball rolling, we strike while the iron's hot.'

Now Gary *did* look a bit animated, at last. In fact, he burst out laughing.

'Just be sure you don't forget to mix your metaphors while you're at it,' he quipped.

It took a good second or two before the penny dropped. But I didn't care. I was at last making some progress.

# Chapter 11

The progress continued into the following week. Which was incredibly satisfying; there was nothing quite like learning something, putting it into practice and actually seeing it working before your eyes, and that was exactly what was happening with Imogen. I continued putting her on the spot, just as I'd been doing the previous week, and, as if by magic, it invariably produced speech. It was as if she was locked in a battle between being the object of scrutiny and getting words out of her mouth and, in the controlled setting we'd chosen, at least, fear of being on the spot was winning out every time.

Better still, Kelly had rearranged much of her timetable so that I could start working on the stimulus withdrawal theory, and this was also working a treat. You could see the anxiety on Imogen's face when asked to speak when Kelly was present also, but I stuck to my guns.

We'd started with small steps: first a question that required only a yes or no response, and at the start of the week I'd allowed her just to nod or shake her head. And as the week progressed, we progressed too. So much so that, by Thursday, I had a plan to take a further step, and try and coax more than one-word answers out of her.

We were doing art, as part of our ongoing quest to encourage self-expression, and today's task was to paint pictures, using only one paint colour, with the colour representing a certain mood. The key thing was for the children, having painted their pictures, to discuss the colour they'd used, what emotion it represented and why they'd chosen it.

I started with Molly, who'd chosen 'sad'. She'd painted a picture using blue paint of a little boy crying. I then moved on to Henry, who'd chosen to do a pirate ship, using black, which he explained was about feeling in a bad mood.

So by the time I got to Imogen, who had painted a picture of a log fire in red, she had an idea of what I expected her to tell me, i.e. something more substantial than a simple yes or a no.

'This is great, Imogen,' I said, clipping her picture up on my big easel. 'And I think I can guess what sort of mood it is you've painted, but, for the rest of the class, can you tell us what it is?'

She lifted her head. 'Angry,' she said quietly.

'Thought so,' I said, smiling. 'And why do you think red shows anger? Is it because when we get into a rage we get all hot and bothered and our blood feels like it's boiling? Or is it perhaps because when people get angry they often say they're "seeing red"? What do you think?'

There was a pause, but, having given her something to

work with now, I waited, and, sure enough, out came three words. 'It's both, Miss.'

She then put her head down, blushing furiously.

I smiled at Kelly. This was going well. This wasn't just supplying a nothing word – this was actively taking part in the lesson. Which meant I could now implement the next part of the strategy, which was to leave the classroom and let Kelly take the rest of the lesson, confident – well, optimistic – that while I was absent she would find the wherewithal to speak to Kelly.

'Baby steps,' I told her, as I grabbed my bag from beneath my desk and prepared to leave them to it. 'But huge leaps, all the same. This will be a red-letter day, if it happens.'

'Oh the pressure,' Kelly replied. 'I shall feel such a failure if I don't get her to speak to me now!'

But, of course, she did. When I returned to the unit, just before lunchtime, having made the most of my half-hour break by sneaking in a coffee and a biscuit, I could tell from Kelly's expression that she had.

They'd been tasked with the business of committing the descriptions of their paintings into a written record in their workbooks and Kelly had been going round from child to child as they did so, reading and checking their work. 'And as I walked round to the girls' table, I took a look and said, "Good work, Imogen," and quick as you like she said thank you! I was – to use your word – totally gobsmacked!'

'That's fabulous,' I said, as I headed towards the kettle so we could grab a coffee as soon as the bell went. 'At this rate we'll have her chatting to all and sundry by Christmas. And you never know – maybe we'll even get her singing carols!'

'Steady on,' cautioned Kelly. 'Rome wasn't built in a day.' But I knew she felt as optimistic as I did. I was already looking forward to the afternoon.

Before that, however, it seemed there would be another development – one that would pull me back to the important fact that it wasn't so much the business of Imogen speaking (vital thought that was) as the business of what she'd have to tell us when she did find her voice.

The boys bundled out, as per usual, within seconds of the lunchtime buzzer and, also as usual, the girls moved at a more leisurely pace. Shona was by nature a calm, organised and methodical girl and, taking her lead – as she had done since they'd both been thrown together – Molly was doing as she did now: organising her backpack with what she'd need for the next hour. Imogen, however, hadn't moved yet. We watched Shona approach her and speak to her, presumably to hurry her along, but when Imogen produced a small plastic lunchbox I realised she wasn't in a hurry to go anywhere.

This was a first. I went over to the girls' table.

'Are you not coming with us?' Molly asked her now, glancing worriedly in my direction. I could almost see her mind working, too, bless her. Trying to work out if she'd done something to offend her. Imogen herself didn't come up with a reply.

'It's fine, girls,' I said, sensing Imogen wanted me to step in. 'Brought a packed lunch in today, then?' I said to Imogen. 'Shall Molly and Shona go ahead, then? It's fine for you to take it to the dining hall, if you want to, but if you want to stay and have it here, that's fine too today. Because I'm going to have my lunch in here today as well.'

This was clearly the answer she was after. Perhaps this lunchbox development would become the norm now – it would at least give her breathing space from the pressure of having to communicate in her lunch break as well as in class. 'I'll eat here, then,' she answered, confirming what I'd anticipated. Then she bowed her head as per usual and peeled the lid from the box.

'Thanks, girls,' I said to the other two. 'You'd better hurry off now, or you'll end up spending half the lunch hour in the queue.'

They did so, and, as Imogen had now pulled out her reading book, I headed back to where Kelly was, at the desk.

'Got your sandwiches, then?' she asked, grinning at me as she slung her bag over her shoulder.

'I wish,' I said. 'But you know what it's like. You just can't get the staff.'

I was always full of good intentions on the 'bring a sandwich in and save money' front, me, but they never got further than exactly that – intentions. 'I tell you what,' I said. 'Any chance you could grab me something from the vending machine while you're around and about? And I tell you what,' I added softly, as a thought suddenly struck me, 'take your time. Because it occurs to me there might be a reason why Imogen wants to stay put in here today, mightn't there?'

And, as it turned out, there was.

\* \* \*

I made myself a coffee and, as Imogen sat nibbling her sandwich, nose in book, I pondered this development and what it meant. Imogen had always gone to lunch with Shona and Molly. That had been a constant. Every single day. So this business of bringing in a sandwich – what did it mean? Assuming it *did* mean anything more than just school-meals refusal, then it would be something she had planned in advance. Of course, it could just be that her nan was on a money saving/healthy eating/change of routine kick, but were that the case then I was fairly sure Imogen already knew that she could take her packed lunch and eat it in the hall.

No, there was a reason behind this. The question was – what should I do? Should I get on with some work, drink my coffee, sit it out till she told me? Or go across to her and ask her if something was bothering her?

The latter, I decided. After all, she had already taken the most difficult step, hadn't she? No, the next step had to come from me.

Those words she had first spoken to me still weighed on my mind. 'I thought she was going to …' What? Come back home to me? Take me with her? Stay in touch? Because I was sure that the 'she' in question must be her absent mother and I was equally sure that this woman – whoever she was – was responsible for Imogen's current trauma. And that was hardly surprising, was it? After all, by all accounts she'd already been the target for bullies, in the way redheads like her – unbelievably, and so cruelly – were. When, exactly, was that ever going to stop? But, on top of that, for her mother to just up and leave like she did, well,

I had little doubt that that would be the straw that had broken the camel's back. How would a child manage to assimilate and cope with such rejection? How *could* they? This was her mother and she'd just disappeared. No wonder the poor kid was so damaged.

But I was about to find out I was wrong. I went to the biscuit tin by the kettle and fished out a couple of biscuits to eat with my coffee. They were probably stale, as I hadn't stocked up in a while, but they'd keep me going till Kelly returned. They'd also make it look less like I was going over to conduct an interrogation and more like we were being companionable over lunch.

I then went over, sat down at the other side of the table, took a bite out of one of the soggy biscuits, then said, 'Mmm, just what I needed. You okay, sweetie?'

The effect was instantaneous. Imogen carefully replaced the uneaten half of her sandwich in her lunchbox, then said, 'No, not really, Miss.'

Just like that. I was stunned. And her big eyes were still on me.

'I understand, love,' I started. 'And I kind of guessed that today. That picture you painted this morning ... All red and angry ... Is it your mum?' I added gently.

She looked confused. And hadn't spoken. Was she going to shut down again?

'Your painting?' I tried again. 'Was that about your mum leaving? I'm sure I'd feel angry too ... You said it represented anger, remember?'

But she was now shaking her head. 'Yes. I mean, no. I mean it's not about my mum.'

'It's not?'

'No. I always kind of knew she would leave.'

Now it was my turn to be confused. Had I got this whole thing completely wrong? 'So that's not what's upsetting you? Your mum and dad splitting up?'

She shook her head again. And now her face began crumpling, her features falling in on themselves.

'Oh, sweetheart, don't cry,' I said, getting up and going round to where Shona usually sat, next to her. 'I'm sorry,' I said, sitting beside her. 'I didn't want to upset you. I just thought that it must be your mum leaving that started this all off. And if it's not … sweetie, you must tell me. If you tell me I might be able to help you.'

'That's just it!' she said, her voice stronger than at any time since she'd come to us. 'You can't help me, Miss. No one can!' She was properly sobbing now so I put an arm round her and pulled her in close. 'It's her!' she said. 'Gerri! She hates me! And I hate her too! And my dad is so *stupid*!' she gulped. 'He thinks the sun shines out of her backside but she's a horrible *witch*!'

I digested all this while I held her. It was an incredible amount to have said and I could tell she'd meant every word of it. So the grandmother was right on that score, at least. Her granddaughter did hate her step-mum. Which was natural in itself. Almost mandatory, sometimes. For taking her dad away? For pushing her out? For merely existing?'

'Oh, sweetheart,' I said. 'You know, I can tell just how much you're hurting. And I know how hard it must be for you, all of it. First your mum leaving and then your dad meeting someone new – aren't adults a pain, eh? And I know how difficult it can be to adjust to all that new stuff. All the changes. Having to get used to this stranger being in your life – specially if you don't agree with dad's choices … but, you know what? Nothing's changed between you and your dad – I *know* that. You will always be his little girl, and he will always love you, and what you have to do is …'

'NO!' The word was shouted, and as Imogen uttered it she pushed me away. 'No!' she repeated, sobbing. 'You're just as bad as my nan and grandad! Nobody ever listens to me! What's the point of talking to anyone if *nobody ever listens to me!*'

It was a shocking and sudden outburst and it seemed she'd done with me. Turning her body away from me she immediately snatched up her book and started pretending to read it. I could tell she wasn't really doing so because her eyes were still so full of tears. But, even so, I had clearly been dismissed.

But the only response was to soldier right on. 'I am so sorry, love,' I tried, speaking mainly to her curtain of hair, 'but if you don't tell me what is wrong, how can I possibly understand? If I have it all wrong then you have to put me right. And I will listen, Imogen. Honestly, I *will*.'

But that, it seemed, was that. I was persona non gratis. She seemed determined to completely ignore me. Blank expression, head down, 'don't come near me' demeanour. An impenetrable shield, but shielding *what*?

I went back to my desk, taking my remaining one and a half soggy biscuits with me, and praying I hadn't completely blown it. That we weren't back to square one as far as speaking was concerned. And I had a good 20 minutes in which to ponder what to do about it, before Kelly breezed back in, bearing a 'Well?' kind of expression, a tuna mayo sandwich and a chocolate bar.

'Greetings!' she announced to the classroom in general. 'I bring a gift from the dinner-lady gods!'

Imogen didn't even lift her head. Not a millimetre.

# Chapter 12

The next couple of days were strained, to say the least. Though Imogen continued to make progress with her mutism in class – answering direct questions from both me and Kelly, and interacting with the rest of the kids to the extent that she'd been doing before, it was as if a light had gone out behind her eyes. Gone were the accompanying smiles I'd begun to enjoy when she spoke to me; now she just looked sullen and slightly hostile and also tired. Defeated, even – as if every day was just something to be got through. And I felt awful, as if it had all been my fault.

I knew that wasn't the full picture and that I should stop beating myself up about it – this was a complicated problem with an as yet undiscovered root. That I hadn't managed to unlock Imogen's one unsolicited utterance – *I thought she was going to* … – was hardly for want of trying, after all. And though she'd been quick to 'punish' me for apparently barking up the wrong tree (something I still wasn't entirely convinced about) I felt even more determined to get to the bottom of whatever was making life so unbearable for this troubled, unhappy girl.

But for all my good intentions, it was difficult to know what best to do next, underlining once again just how hard it was to make progress with the root problem when the symptoms it had caused were such a barrier – no, the *ultimate* barrier – to communication: she couldn't tell us! And I couldn't speak to Gary about it, either. He was away working in one of our feeder schools this week, doing training in child-protection issues.

I'd written up my report, and handed copies to both learning support and Don, the deputy head, but these people were always busy, and had scores of problems requiring their attention at any given time, so I wasn't optimistic that I'd get anything in the way of feedback for at least the next few days. No, I'd just have to hang on, keep the lines of communication open with Imogen, and bend Gary's ears about it once he was back in the following Monday.

But I hadn't factored in Kieron, who gave me a fresh perspective on the problem – one I really should have worked out for myself. It was on the Friday evening, and bar Riley, who was at the cinema with her boyfriend David, we were all sitting down to supper, and I was summing up the frustrations of my week to Mike.

I suspected he wished he'd never asked, but I ploughed on in any case. It was in the marriage vows, wasn't it? Listening to your wife blathering on when she's had a hard time at work? 'So, of course, it feels like it's all my fault,' I was saying, 'that we're back to square one. And I'm really not sure what's the best next step to take.'

'How can it be your fault, Mum?' Kieron wanted to know. 'She hasn't spoken for months, has she? And now she has. So, actually, that's progress, isn't it? Because you've done what you set out to do, haven't you?'

'Ah, would that it were that simple, son,' Mike said, with the sort of grin that indicated that I was about to have the mickey taken out of me. 'See, our little Ms Watson here – no relation to Dr Watson, admittedly, and definitely not to Sherlock Holmes – won't be happy with simply, and single-handedly, completing the job in hand and pausing to give herself a small pat on the back. No, no,' he continued, adopting the sort of portentous voice that put me in mind of the man who did the voiceover for *Hergé's Adventures of Tintin*, 'above and beyond the call of duty! No task too big! No mystery too mysterious! Swoops in on her wings of –'

'Oh, shut UP, Mike!' I said, affecting my snappiest voice, while trying to cuff Kieron round the head for joining in and giggling. 'Eat your bloody meatballs, the pair of you, and be careful not to choke!'

'Oh, Mum, Dad is funny, though – you've got to give him that much.'

'Not *that* funny,' I pointed out, even though it had made me smile. I probably needed to take a step back and stop being so intense about it. I couldn't fix everything in a week – I wasn't God, for goodness' sake. And it was the weekend. I should probably lighten up.

'Seriously, though,' Kieron continued, the bit obviously between his teeth now. 'If you think the problem with this girl is all about wife number one, why don't you go and ask wife number two? After all, according to Dad there's nothing most women love more than telling tales on other women.'

'I never said that! Well, not exactly, anyway,' Mike said, as I glared at him.

'Actually, Kieron,' I said, 'that's not a half bad idea. She probably could share some light on things, couldn't she? And would probably be happy to, since Imogen's apparently given her so much grief. And I've only spoken to the grandparents so far … no, you're right. It would be a good idea to widen the net a bit, wouldn't it?'

Kieron guffawed. 'Widen the net? Mum, you're priceless!'

I shooed the pair of them away into the living room as soon as supper was done with and, as it had been Kieron who'd been on lay-the-table-and-dish-up duty, set about the clearing away and washing up. Strictly speaking, this was supposed to be Riley's job this evening, but as they'd gone to an earlyish screening – she'd had her food before us – she had left with the traditional Riley pronouncement to 'Just leave it all and I'll sort it once I'm back.'

She knew full well, of course, that I could no more do this than fly, on account of my 'thing', to use the technical term, about mess and disorder. I'd never been any different, and doubted that I ever would, either – and it sometimes struck me that perhaps I was the root cause of several of Kieron's funny little ways. He too, hated disorder, which was probably connected to his Asperger's, but might also be in part his genetic inheritance. Either way, he'd always been a child who looked after his belongings and woe betide anyone who disturbed any of his carefully arranged books or toys. Indeed, Riley soon learned the art of targeted teasing, and would play pranks on him for no more important reason than it allowed her to watch him go slightly mad for a while. (Which, thinking about it, was a perfectly valid reason, because that was what being siblings was sometimes all about.)

Despite some of his odd ways, though, Kieron was a simple child in many ways, tending to see things in black and white. He still did and, of course, that was what he'd done now. Where I'd wrestle with a problem for several days, he could on occasion nail the logic before anyone else did. And he was right. I had succeeded in getting Imogen to speak, which was progress, and this wobble was really just a step on the journey. And of course I should see if I could speak to the second Mrs Hinchcliffe, I thought, as I put the dishes away. I should perhaps have tried to do that from the off.

'Excellent progress!' Gary said, when I went to see him on the Monday morning, straight after registration, leaving Kelly to hold the fort. 'Seriously,' he added, 'I don't know how much you've read around the whole trauma-based type of selective mutism, but after I did I was seriously concerned that we'd fail to get anywhere, because once it becomes entrenched as a coping mechanism it can apparently get progressively worse. So, yes, this is great news. Well done.'

I had read that and had chosen not to dwell on it. I said so. 'And I'm still not sure I'd be that excited *just* yet,' I added. 'It feels more like one step forward, two steps back at the moment. And I'm still convinced there's some deep-seated issue around the departure of her mother. Which is mostly why I'm here. I know they're not her current guardians, but I was wondering if the head would sanction a visit to Imogen's dad and step-mum – assuming they'll talk to me, that is. After all, we still don't have anything like a full picture of why she ended up with her nan and grandad in the first place. It's all a bit vague, that, don't you think?'

Gary nodded. 'I can't see any reason why he wouldn't,' he agreed. 'Though perhaps it's best if the approach comes from me. If they're at all reluctant – and I've a hunch they might be, given that they've voluntarily relinquished care of his only daughter, however "challenging" she's been – my role in school will give the request added weight.'

'As it should,' I agreed. 'She's clearly not thriving in the world at present, is she? What parent wouldn't want to be supported by the school in trying to achieve that?'

'Exactly,' said Gary. 'So leave it with me. I'm assuming one day straight after school would suit you best, yes?'

I told him it would and, after grabbing a quick cup of coffee, hurried back to the Unit. The kids were in good spirits, full of chatter about what they'd got up to on their weekends, and settling companionably to their work while I got the wall boards up to date with the work we'd completed on the Friday. All apart from Imogen, that was, who was still monosyllabic. I was clearly no longer flavour of the month.

There was good news, however, within a scant couple of hours, as it seemed Gary had had no problem getting hold of Gerri Hinchcliffe, Imogen's nan being only too pleased to pass on her son and daughter-in-law's number, in the hope that some progress could be made.

'And if you're free straight after school today,' he added, 'you're apparently welcome to pop round there. Imogen's dad won't be there himself, but I figured you'd rather see her sooner rather than later, right? Otherwise, he'll be back end of this week. Working away or something?'

I nodded. 'He's a coach driver. And you're right,' I said, Imogen's stony face coming immediately to mind. 'Sooner is definitely better than later. And, to be honest, it might be better seeing Gerri on her own, in any case. I think she'll be much more likely to open up about how Imogen's been with her – not to mention the whole business of the first wife running off – without him there to censor her at all, don't you?'

'I think you're probably right. Though she did say she won't have that long. Got to take a cat to a vet or something. But I assured her it was only a quick chat you were after. Anyway, Sherlock, report back tomorrow and let me know how you got on, okay?'

Tsk. Him as well now. I was beginning to wonder if I shouldn't get myself a deerstalker and start smoking a pipe.

For all my enthusiasm for visiting Imogen's dad and stepmum, however, by the time the bell went at the end of the day a few mild misgivings had begun to creep in. For one thing I felt a bit sneaky. Yes, it was perfectly acceptable for me – or any other member of staff, for that matter – to speak to parents and/or guardians of troubled pupils without consulting them, because you did what you needed to do to help the child. But in this case I had the sense that if I put Imogen in the picture I might just inflame things all over again. She'd called her step-mum a 'witch', after all, so I didn't doubt she'd have her own view on my going to talk to her.

Which I could at least rationalise. Step-mums routinely got a bad press, both in fairy tales and in real life, and if you believed everything you heard from kids in the middle of acrimonious break-ups you'd think being a stepmother made you the devil incarnate, almost by default. Which didn't seem to be borne out by the facts in this particular family – Imogen's grandparents had made that very clear.

But my other misgiving was more niggling and less readily countered. What was my plan exactly? What was I going to ask her when I got there? There was a fine line between gentle probing to try and glean a fuller picture, and interfering – for want of a less pejorative term – in someone's life. And perhaps the business of her predecessor leaving was the last thing she wanted to talk about. And wasn't I making a bit of an unwarranted assumption about how much she actually even knew?

Oh well, I thought, climbing into my car and pulling my road atlas out. It was done now. I was expected. And I would learn something of value, surely? In for a penny and all that …

The younger Hinchcliffes lived in a small, terraced house on a newish estate about half an hour's drive from the school. It had a neat but plain-looking front garden –

square of grass, concrete path, nothing more – and there were businesslike vertical blinds at all the windows, half opened to let in light but maintain privacy.

The front door was opened by a slim, thirty-something-looking blonde woman, with pearl earrings, an expression of very mild agitation and, in her arms, an enormous white cat.

'*So* nice to meet you, Mrs Watson,' she enthused, nevertheless, indicating a door just behind her that I should go through. 'Your colleague did tell you, though, didn't he, that I'm on something of a tight schedule? I have to take Flynn here to the vets in half an hour.'

'Yes, he did,' I reassured her, as she followed me into a warm, woody sitting room. 'Nothing serious, I hope?'

'No, no, just a jab,' she explained, nuzzling her face into the cat's fluffy neck. It had long hair, and masses of it, too. 'Flynn and Grace, there' – she tilted her head towards another giant cat, curled up in front of a roaring coal fire – 'they're both show cats. Won all kinds of awards between them,' she added proudly, 'and of course we travel all over the country with them – well, I do mainly, as Graham's so often tied up with work – and they do tend to pick up the odd sniffle, as you'd expect, as they're constantly mixing with other cats. So you can't be too careful.'

'I imagine not,' I agreed, sitting down on the sofa, following her invitation, while she perched on the edge of the armchair opposite. 'And I suppose they're more vulnerable, being pedigrees.'

'Well, exactly,' she said. 'Weak immune systems, that's the main thing we're up against.'

To which I wanted to reply 'All that in-breeding, I suppose' but felt it perhaps wouldn't go down too well. Because this was someone who took her cat shows quite seriously, was my analysis – which wasn't even much of one, because it really didn't need to be. There was evidence enough all around me. Most obviously, there was a display cabinet not three feet away, which was stuffed with photographs, rosettes and a variety of framed certificates as well as a selection of cups and trophies big and small. Moreover, everything my eyes rested upon gleamed as if regularly polished, as did the clutch of framed photos that were clustered on the shelf below, which at a glance seemed to be of their wedding.

'So,' said Mrs Hinchcliffe brightly, 'how *can* I help you, Mrs Watson? I know there have been some ongoing difficulties with Im, from what your colleague was saying. So she's *still* refusing to talk to anyone?'

I nodded. 'Well, the odd word or two, but, no, sadly, we've not been able to make as much progress as we'd have liked.'

'It's such a shame,' Mrs Hinchcliffe said, shaking her head, while still methodically stroking the cat on her lap. 'We were all so hopeful that a change of school might do the trick …' She sighed heavily. 'So. Clearly not, then.'

'That's why I'm here,' I went on. 'Because I thought you might be able to shed a little further light on the background. What we're most keen to get to is the root to all this –'

'Oh, dear,' she said. 'In which case, you've probably come to the wrong person. As I said to your colleague, I'm not sure what I can contribute to all this, because where discipline's concerned Graham and I have decided I'm better off keeping my distance.' She frowned. 'A long story, but an all too familiar one, sadly. Damned if you do and damned if you don't, eh? I'm sure you've seen this sort of thing before.'

'Well, yes, I have,' I agreed, 'but this isn't really about discipline, Mrs Hinchcliffe. Imogen's no trouble in school at all, it's that –'

'Oh, pur-*lease* call me Gerri,' she said. 'Mrs Hinchcliffe makes me feel so *old*!'

'Sorry – Gerri, then, and, as I say, it's not a discipline issue. Imogen's never been less than well behaved. And it's not that she hasn't made *some* progress. It's just that the specialist who's been to see us to tell us more about selective mutism has told us that if we can establish some possible causes of Imogen's difficulty, we will be much better placed to help her deal with it.'

'Selective mutism – so it has a name then?'

'Indeed it does.'

'I didn't know that,' she answered, 'though, of course, that does make sense. And I'm more than happy to help in any way I can, Mrs Watson. No doubt about it, that child has given me no end of problems, but I'm intelligent enough to know that it's all down to her mother – she just can't help but resent me, can she? Because I'm not her and will never be.' She sighed. 'So. What exactly can I help you *with*?'

The cat on her lap, Flynn, launched himself off it at that moment and she jumped up and began brushing hairs from her clothes. 'Now that's the only downside,' she said, smiling down indulgently at the mewing animal. 'What?' she asked it, continuing to pick fluff from her (rather impractical, to my mind) black trousers. 'What is it you *want*, Flynnie-boy?'

Since he wasn't about to answer, I could only sit and suppress my urge to grin. 'I'm so sorry,' she then said, scooping the cat back into her arms again. 'I haven't even offered you a drink. What can I get you?'

I shook my head. 'I'm fine,' I said. Then, having thought about it, said, 'Actually, I wouldn't mind a glass of water.'

'Of course,' she said brightly. 'Won't be a tick.'

I took advantage of her absence to take a closer look at the cabinet, which, close up, really was stuffed with prizes and plaudits. But I was altogether more interested in the wedding photos. I loved looking at people's wedding photos, and these were no exception. And very exotic-looking wedding photos they were too. It had obviously taken place on a beach – somewhere with plenty of swaying palm trees – and both these and exotic flowering shrubs were very much in evidence, right down to the hibiscus blooms in the bride's bouquet and hair. I was also struck by how readily I was able to identify Imogen's father. He had the same red hair, though his was close cropped and lightly receding, and the same attractive wide-set blue eyes.

'Beautiful, aren't they?' Gerri said as she came back into the sitting room. 'That one on the right there? That was Grace when she won best in breed at her last show. She'll be going for a triple in a fortnight – quite the little supermodel!'

I took the proffered water, and this time didn't feel quite the same urge to smile at her assumption that I'd been absorbed in the fêted cats. 'Yes, they are,' I agreed anyway. 'You must be very proud. Anyway ...'

'Yes, yes,' she agreed. 'But, as with everything, there's an element of luck in these shows. Mind you,' she added, clearly on a subject that was close to her heart, 'it's not *all* down to luck. There's a lot of prep involved as well. Sometimes the difference between a silver and a gold can be the tiniest margin, as you can imagine. And that's what I *am* good at,' she finished, smiling fondly towards the cabinet. 'Attention. Attention to all those tiny little details. Anyway,' she said, claping her hands together. 'Time is short, of course. So fire away.'

I duly fired. 'Well,' I said, 'it's really just a question of you giving me some background. As much as you're able to, of course ...'

'About Imogen's mother? Well, what I suppose I *can* say is that she wasn't any sort of mother. From what I can gather, anyway,' she added, shaking her head. 'As I'm sure Graham's mother has already told you, he slaved all the hours God gave him, but it was never enough – not for Miss Fancy Pants. No, sad to say, as soon as a man with a larger pay packet came along, she was off with him like a shot. Graham was relieved, I know, but you can imagine, can't you? She left the poor child reeling, and – sad to relate – I think Im blamed her father; she took it out on him, certainly, and then, when *I* came along – well, you can imagine, can't you? Our getting together only served to make her worse. I tried everything, of course I did, but there was never any getting through to her, and, well' – she lifted both hands, palms upwards – 'what can you *do*? She decided I was the enemy, and that, I'm afraid, was that.'

'And that was when she moved in with her grandparents?'

The other cat, Grace, left her spot by the fire, and came and wound herself around my legs. 'Ah, she likes you,' Gerri gushed. 'And she's *very* discriminating. Are you a cat person, Mrs Watson?'

'Not currently,' I said, smiling. 'We're in a pet-free period at the moment. My teenagers keep me busy enough, to be honest! So Imogen wanted to go?' I asked, trying to get her back on track again. 'You know, to move out and move in with your husband's parents?'

'I'm not entirely sure,' she said. 'It was Graham's idea initially – you know, just for all of us to have some time out. It was so difficult for him, wanting to be loyal to her, but seeing what it was doing to me.' She looked directly at me. 'It was extremely difficult, Mrs Watson,' she said in a voice that seemed suddenly full of emotion. 'Some of the things she used to call me, the lies she'd tell about me ... And, of course, you have to bite your lip and just take it, don't you? What else *can* you do in my kind of situation? And I think Graham ...' she trailed off, and I wondered if she was going to cry. She was clearly upset.

'Could see how much it was distressing you?' I asked her. 'I don't doubt it. And from what I've heard from his parents, it sounds as though you had it pretty tough ...'

'Which is not to say I ever wanted *that* to happen,' she said. 'For Im to leave us. Far from it. I only ever wanted to help her. But in the end I think we *all* felt that, well … perhaps *space* was what was needed. And that perhaps she was better off where she was. And, of course, by this time she'd started all this sudden not-speaking business, which was distressing for Graham too, because he felt he'd lost her, that he'd *failed* her …' She blinked at me. Seemed to gather herself. 'So now we're all at sea, aren't we? I mean, what *can* we do? If her mother would only …' She stood up now and brushed her trousers down again. It seemed an action so automatic that she wasn't even aware of doing it. 'If only – hark at me! That's not going to happen, is it? Anyway …'

'Yes, of course,' I said, rising and looking for a surface on which I could put my glass.

She took it and sighed. 'I've not been a great help to you, have I?'

'Yes, you have,' I said. *No*, I thought, *you haven't. Not very much*.

But then, perhaps she couldn't be. Imogen had clearly taken against her, or, at the very least, taken against the *idea* of her. Nothing unfamiliar there. Perhaps the problem was that Imogen wasn't a 'cat person'. Whatever else she was, she certainly seemed a little flaky. But whatever the ins and outs of the current travails in this family, my principal feeling as I waved and drove off was that I'd just been an extra in some bizarre play.

# Chapter 13

What was it about Gerri Hinchcliffe? The question vexed me. She had been unfailingly nice, unfailingly polite, unfailingly ... what? Unfailingly correct. Yes, that was probably the word for it. Correct, neat and tidy – if a touch Stepford-Wifey – and though self-pitying enough to be ever so slightly irritating, not so much that I felt justified in holding it against her. After all, she had never even been 'the other woman' in this scenario. She hadn't 'stolen' Imogen's dad away from her mother, as Imogen herself might have seen it. She had just walked into an already unhappy family situation. Imogen's mother had left her father long before.

Of course, it could have been that, unbeknown to everyone, she'd been having an affair with him all along, but the facts didn't fit and, well, even if they had, it wasn't for me to pass judgement on Imogen's father's love life, was it? My role was quite specific but at the same time quite general: to try and help children to reach a place where they could thrive in their new circumstances, whatever they were. And there were many children in situations like Imogen's, after all.

Oh, but what *was* it about Gerri Hinchcliffe? It was a question I took home with me and pondered all that evening, eventually falling into a fitful, erratic sleep; periods of wakefulness punctuated by half-realised dreams involving wicked step-mothers, witches and other fairy-tale staples, all of which berated me for venturing opinions about them – *damned if you do*, as Gerri Hinchcliffe had said, *and damned if you don't*.

It was almost four in the morning when it hit me. I'd woken up for what must have been the third or fourth time, and turned over, as I habitually did, to see what the time was, so I could calculate what the chances were of getting back to sleep before the alarm put an end to it either way.

The display read 03.57, glowing red in the darkness, emitting enough light to illuminate something else. It was as familiar a thing to me as everything else in my bedroom – a double photo-frame I'd had sitting there for quite a few years now, from which Kieron, to the left, and Riley, to the right, grinned goofy, self-conscious school-photo smiles.

I'd bought the frame years back – and chosen the photos to go in it – to take away on a residential course with me, back when I was working with vulnerable young people. It had been a big thing for me, going away on that week-long course, because it was the first time I'd spent so long away from my children since either had been born.

I looked at the kids' faces now, in the darkness, and that was when it hit me. *That* was the thing about Gerri

Hinchcliffe, I decided. That in her home – in the home she shared with Imogen's dad – I didn't see a single photograph of Imogen.

Big ideas at four in the morning don't always seem quite as big in the cold light of day, but in the murky autumnal light of the next morning I realised, as I hurried from home to school, that, on balance, this one did have legs.

Yes, I'd only been in the sitting room, so I obviously couldn't speak for the rest of the house, but this was a sitting room stuffed to bursting with mementoes. As well as the cabinet full of the various spoils of pedigree-cat war, it was a room that wasn't light on ornamentation. I couldn't bring much in the way of specifics to mind now, but the overall impression had been one of a room in which all the knick-knacks meant something. And then there were the wedding pictures, and they were what had really sprung to mind, for within them – and there were about six of them on the shelf – there had not been a single one that contained Imogen. Had she even been there? That was what I most wanted to know.

So, given that I still had ten minutes before the bell went for registration, I went to the staffroom, made a coffee, then took myself off to the adjoining quiet room, which as well as couple of computer terminals had two external phones, one of which I used to telephone Imogen's nan.

I had intended calling her anyway, just to thank her for paving the way so that I could speak to her son and daughter-in-law, and just to let her know that I had been round to visit Gerri. That much was a simple courtesy, and a chance to continue to build on good relations, but now I had a more pressing reason to get her on the phone; I wanted an answer to my as yet unspoken question.

'Hello, dear,' she said, managing to convey with two words how heavy was the weight currently on her shoulders. 'How are things with Imogen in school this week?'

I filled her in on such progress as we'd been able to make, and was disappointed to hear our small increments of positivity weren't matched by any change in her emotional well-being at home. Which I tried to steer away from, as I'd pretty much reached the conclusion that nothing would change all the while we hadn't got to the bottom of whatever had caused the mutism in the first place. All I knew was that I wasn't buying the bullying at school angle; not when there was a new potential angle bedding down in my head now, unsubstantiated but there nevertheless.

I spent a minute or two discussing Gerri and her facility with showing cats, and once again I heard nothing but praise. So I stepped lightly into the territory of the absence of photos, conscious that loyalties very much needed to be respected.

'Oh, and something I forgot to ask,' I added chattily, aware this could be sensitive ground. 'Your son's wedding. I saw the pictures. It looked lovely ... did Imogen go? Only I saw some of the photographs, but no sign of Imogen being bridesmaid, and I wondered ...'

'No, you wouldn't,' said Mrs Hinchcliffe, without any hint of edge. 'She wasn't there. Not really feasible, what with them having it abroad and everything – Graham got such a good deal on a package through one of his contacts at the tour operators, it seemed silly not to. So we looked after her. Money was tight, and it wasn't really that sort of wedding. They didn't want to make a big fuss of it, for obvious reasons …'

'Of course,' I agreed. 'Yes, of course.'

I put the phone down feeling something akin to a hair-on-the-back-of-the-neck prickle. Again, of itself, it was no big thing, really. Lots of people getting married for the second time did things in the same way. Small, unfussy wedding, no big occasion, no pomp and circumstance. So why did something about this one feel so wrong? It was just a simple tying of the knot, after all – and perhaps Imogen hadn't even *wanted* to be there. She clearly hadn't wanted to be landed with a step-mum, had she? And I had heard from her own lips that she hadn't wanted to be landed with *this* step-mum. She had been happy as she was – just her and her dad. She'd been his princess, and now perhaps she felt she'd been usurped. Perhaps she made a big fuss about *not* being there to witness it.

It was a familiar enough scenario, trying to 'blend' a family in that way; one that would have needed tact and sensitivity, so that the child – in this case Imogen – didn't feel pushed out. And perhaps they'd all tried their best – they certainly seemed to think they had – but *had* they?

Try as I might, I just couldn't talk myself out of the feeling that, actually, the evidence was beginning to tell me something different. Which made it doubly frustrating that Imogen couldn't – or more correctly, now, *wouldn't* – talk to me.

I made my way back to the Unit feeling that frustration very keenly. I *had* to get that child to open up.

Imogen wasn't the only child in the Unit, however, and though the morning passed peacefully and harmoniously enough, by the time the lunchtime bell went it became clear that this happy state of affairs wouldn't continue, as Gavin hadn't brought in his midday pill.

ADHD was a condition that was frustrating for all, but in Gavin's case, so far, things had been reasonably well managed, in that he was generally responsible enough to do what was required of him, i.e. take his morning pill with breakfast and bring his second into school, which he would leave with the medical room, ready to go and take as soon as the lunchtime bell went.

I didn't get involved in this arrangement. The deal since day one had been that Gavin himself would take responsibility; it was part of the package of strategies that had been agreed when he was moved into the Unit for assessment. It was also one of the ways he could prove to the school generally that he was responsible about managing his difficulties.

But there was no doubt that being on Ritalin wasn't a universal panacea. I'd had dealings with kids on Ritalin more than once over the years, and there was one constant – it came up regularly, both in my experience and from what I'd read. Where the world when unmedicated was kind of 'spiky', like a heart-monitor trace, all zig-zags of highs and lows, with the drug the spikes became more of a flat line – while not exactly level, certainly reduced to a smoother, flatter route, with the result that the world became a 'whateva' kind of place. It wasn't uncommon, therefore, for kids to 'forget' their meds or pretend they had taken them when they hadn't, just so they could 'feel'.

I didn't think for a moment that Gavin had forgotten his pill on purpose, not least because he was the one to tell me. Yes, that was prudent, because the information would have filtered to me in any case, but his explanation – some complex story involving a crying sibling and a dead goldfish – was delivered in such a way that immediately rang true.

And it was too late to do anything much about it. I knew Gavin's mum worked, so it was unlikely that she'd be able to get it to us – she'd have to leave work, travel home and then make another trip to us with it, by which time it would probably be way too late. 'So,' I said to Gavin, 'you will just have to be very Zen-like this afternoon, won't you?'

'What's a Zen?' he wanted to know.

'It's not an "a",' I said, 'it's a religion. One that's all about sitting quietly, thinking deep important thoughts.' I took his hands and clasped them together as if in prayer. 'Kind of like this,' I said, chanting 'Tomorrow I will remember my pill, tomorrow I will remember my pill ...'

Which had sent him away giggling, but the minute we got back into class I could tell there wouldn't be much sitting around, going 'om' a lot, happening. In fact, we were on course for a bit of a nightmare; though Gavin wasn't literally bouncing off the walls, he was definitely doing his Duracell bunny impression, and very quickly getting on everyone's nerves. Had Kelly been around it was one of those situations where I'd have had her take him out and engage him in some focused one-to-one time, but with two TAs off sick she was having to assist in another class-room, so it was going to be a case of crisis containment, i.e. minimising his effect on the group as a whole. But it was proving difficult.

We were kicking off with life-space interviews that after-noon, and, Imogen's being necessarily fairly short, she'd already been 'done' and dispatched to the quiet corner. I was now trying to chat to Shona, but it was proving rather challenging. Despite regular quiet reminders that 'work quietly' meant just that, it seemed Gavin just couldn't help himself. 'Miss!' called Molly for the fifth time in as many minutes. 'Gavin's kicking my chair again.'

'And he's stolen my pencil sharpener as well, Miss!' Henry huffed. 'Gavin, you spaz, give it *back*!'

'Miss, Henry said spastic!' piped up Ben. 'Tell him off, Miss!'

'No I didn't, you liar!' Henry shouted. 'I said spaz!'

'It's the same, isn't it, Miss? Spaz means the same as spas-tic, doesn't it?'

'Boys!' I said sharply. 'Enough of this childish bickering! I don't want to hear *either* word said in this class. And Gavin, will you please stop kicking Molly's chair, *now*. And if you have *borrowed* Henry's pencil sharpener, will you please give it back.'

Naturally, Gavin, Ritalin-free, couldn't simply return it. No, he lobbed it at Henry, whereupon it bounced off his head.

'Oi, you retard!' said Henry. 'Miss, did you see that? He threw it at me!'

'Miss,' piped up Ben, 'Henry called Gavin a retard!'

And off we all went once again.

Exchanging a look of exasperation with poor bemused Shona, I left her at my desk and went over to sort things out. 'Right,' I said, 'Molly, I suggest you go and sit in Shona's seat, out of kicking distance, and Ben and Henry, will you please just concentrate on your *own* work and stop this endless bickering. You're not in flipping primary school! And as for you, Gavin, I would like you to get your reading book out, and –'

'I forgot it, Miss,' he said, drumming two pencils on the desk.

I placed a hand on top of them. 'In which case,' I said, 'I would like you to go to the book corner and choose a different one. And once you've chosen – and *don't* bother Imogen while you're in there – bring it over to me, quietly, along with a chair. Then, once I've finished what I'm doing with Shona, you and I will read it together.'

Gavin got up, scraped his chair back, and hoicked up his trousers.

'Is he getting told off, Miss?' he said, pointing an accusing finger at Henry. 'Cos he's called me a spaz *and* a retard now.'

I pointed a finger of my own. 'Gavin, book corner. *Now*, please,' I told him. And in a tone that left no room for debate, so he didn't offer any. Instead, glaring at Henry, he stomped off.

But if I thought that would contain things, albeit temporarily, I was wrong. Within seconds of my returning to my desk and chat with Shona, the air was rent by a loud and piercing scream.

And, surprise, surprise, it was coming from the book corner.

'Honestly!' I began, stomping over to see what was happening behind the bookcase, 'I give you one simple thing to do, Gavin, and you can't even do *that* without – what on earth!' I finished, 'Stop this right *now*!'

I probably wouldn't have believed it had I not seen it with my own eyes, but Gavin and Imogen were engaged in a physical fight on the book-corner beanbags. I had no idea what had started it, only that I would very quickly need to finish it, as they were laying into each other hell for leather. And, as I went to welly in, Gavin managed to wrestle a book from Imogen's hands – presumably the trophy he'd had his eye on all along.

*Good*, I thought, making a grab for Gavin – at least I wouldn't have to haul him off her bodily. In terms of size, he was way bigger and stronger than she was, and only half an inch shorter than me. But in terms of sheer temper, she had the edge over him. And it seemed she didn't care for having her battles fought for her, because even as I got a grip on Gavin's other wrist she had lunged at him, reaching for the book, which he now waggled tantalisingly out of reach.

'Give it back, you fucking bastard,' she roared, 'or I'll fucking punch your face in!'

You could almost hear the astonished gasp from the small crowd of onlookers, while, unbalanced by her cannoning into a now startled Gavin, I stumbled on the corner of a beanbag and lost my grip on his wrist.

'Yeah, just try it, ginge!' he retaliated, waving the open book in the air above her, before darting past me and across to the other side of the boys' desk, where Henry and Ben were already exchanging smirks, full of glee at the unexpected floor-show.

'*Gavin!*' I snapped, following him. 'Give me that at *once!*'

'That book's *mine!*' Imogen screamed at him, bowling past me to get to him. 'I'm going to fucking kill you, you hear me, dickhead? It's *mine!*'

Gavin was light on his feet though and dodged her again, and, seemingly not satisfied with the commotion he'd caused that far, then – for reasons that escaped me, and probably him, too – ripped a handful of pages out and flung them at her for good measure.

It was cartoonish in its stupidity, but at the same time deadly serious; he clearly couldn't have chosen a better action to enrage her. I could see the expression on her face change as she watched the pages flutter floorwards; then she spun around, grabbed the classroom door handle and, with a howl, fled the room.

I looked across at Gavin with a kind of stunned incredulity. *Yup. I have definitely lost control here*, I thought.

Thank heavens, then, for a man with impeccable timing. 'Everything okay, Mrs Watson?' came a voice. It was Gary. 'Only I just saw Imogen –'

'Ah, Mr Clark,' I puffed, panting and extremely grateful. I had no idea which deity had arranged for him to be at the right place at the right time, but I sent up a blanket prayer of thanks. 'Yes,' I said, nodding towards the corridor, 'do you think you could go after her?'

'Right away,' he said, giving me a thumbs up. 'Don't worry. I'll grab her. Take her to my office. Oh, and I'll send along Miss Vickers.'

Then he was gone.

'Wow, that's a *voice*!' observed Henry.

# Chapter 14

'Right, guys, time to settle down,' I announced, raising my voice above the growing din. Scuffles were ten a penny but Imogen's colourful vocal contribution was a first, and with the tension now dissipated everyone seemed to have something to say – not least, as Henry seemed keen to point out, that mild-mannered Imogen knew three whole swear words.

Everyone, that was, bar Gavin. He had slumped down in his seat with the demeanour of a condemned man – or at least one who, the adrenalin rush finally over and done with, is thinking, 'Oops, might have gone a bit far, there.' Still, I thought, feeling an unexpected rush of sympathy for him, at least he'd been stunned into temporary silence.

I clapped my hands together twice to underline what I'd said. 'Settle down, back to seats, quieten down now, okay?'

'What about Imogen, Miss?' Molly asked, looking concerned.

'I'll go and check on Imogen as soon as Miss Vickers gets here,' I reassured her. 'In the meantime, I want you all to choose a book from the book corner – one at a time, please. Go on, Henry, you first. And then read them *quietly*, okay?'

Kelly was there in less time than it took them all to do so, by which time I'd picked up the pages Gavin had ripped from Imogen's book, as well as the book itself, which lay tented in the middle of the classroom floor, where he'd dropped it, like the proverbial hot brick. As I'd half-realised from the cover illustration, it was the book Imogen had been reading at home – the Jacqueline Wilson one about the twins who'd lost their mother. A book that presumably meant a great deal to her, judging by her reaction to Gavin taking it. I glanced across at him. *Why?* I thought. Why do that? Just to tease her? Just to provoke precisely that kind of reaction? Well, if so, he certainly succeeded.

'Did Gary manage to find her?' I asked Kelly as I stuffed the book and pages into my satchel.

She nodded. 'She was only by the water fountain, apparently. She's up there with him now.'

'Right, then, I'll get over there,' I said, 'and leave you to it. I'll deal with Gavin later, but right now I'm hoping that as her dander's well and truly up, she'll have something more to say for herself. I've never seen her quite like that. She was livid. And very, how shall I put it? Expressive.'

I grinned. 'But I dare say this lot will fill you in.'

Kelly winked at Henry. 'I don't doubt that. Do you?'

I made it up to Gary's office just before the bell went for afternoon break, to find the door to his room wide open, and Imogen seated at the large desk that ran along the far wall. It had two computer terminals along it and she was seated at one of them, typing something steadily and rhythmically.

Gary himself was standing behind and slightly to the side of her, and as soon as he became aware that I'd come into the office he put a finger to his lip before beckoning me across. I slipped my bag from my shoulder and put it down quietly. Whatever she was doing she was clearly very focused, because she'd made no move to suggest she was even aware of Gary, let alone that I'd entered the room. She still looked angry – her skin flushed, her plaits sprouting hair from her tussle – but oblivious to everything around her.

Gary said nothing but pointed to the keyboard, which he seemed to be scrutinising with great concentration. He was presumably trying to work out what she was typing, I realised, because what belatedly struck me was most surprising of all – the monitor wasn't even switched on. *What's she typing?* he mouthed at me, once I'd taken in what was happening, as she continued to bang away at the keys. I watched her too, more analytically, till I could see what Gary obviously could – that she seemed to be repeating the same sequence over and over again.

Gary stepped back, then, just enough that he'd be sufficiently out of earshot so that when he whispered 'I think I've got it', she wouldn't hear. He reached for paper, then, while I continued to watch her fingers move across the keyboard. She was only using two and she wasn't typing too fast for me to follow, so when Gary handed me a bit of paper on which he'd written what he thought it was I already knew what it was going to say.

*I thought she was going to set fire to me.*

The words seemed to leap from the page. *Finally*, the answer to the riddle of what she'd tried to say to me all those days ago. And, if we were right – and we both continued to watch, just to be sure we were – then my suggestions had all been *way* off-beam. Set fire to her? When? And *why*, for that matter? And, most pressingly of all, I thought, *who?*

I became aware of Gary's arm touching my own. 'I need to get to a meeting,' he said quietly, though not so quietly Imogen wouldn't hear him now – after all, we'd divined what we needed to know. 'Can I leave you to it?'

'Of course,' I said, pulling a chair up beside Imogen. 'You get off. We'll see you later. Imogen,' I said then, placing the piece of paper beside the keyboard. 'Imogen, look, sweetheart. Mr Clark's written it down – see? What you've been typing. That's what it was, wasn't it? See? We've worked it out.'

She glanced fleetingly at the piece of paper and then carried on typing. Then she looked again, and this time her fingers came to rest. She slid them down into her lap and clasped them together.

I could tell from the slight movements in her shoulders that she was crying, so I put my arm around her and pulled her close. She didn't stiffen, which I took to be a positive. But neither did she react in any other way. 'Sweetheart,' I said again, 'please tell me how I can help you. Who did you think was going to set fire to you?'

I almost added 'Was it your mum?' but stopped myself in time. Instinct was by now telling me that wasn't going to be the answer anyway. Instinct was telling me it was going to be someone else. 'Imogen,' I said next, 'was it Gerri?'

She seemed to deflate then, like a balloon that had been pricked at a party, shrinking down into herself before pulling her back straight, and wiping tears from her eyes with the backs of her index fingers. Then she nodded. 'It was Gerri,' she confirmed.

'Did she hurt you? Did she burn you? What happened, love? Can you tell me?'

She shook her head. 'No, Miss,' she said, 'she didn't actually burn me, but she said she would. I *thought* she would …' She shuddered then, and the tears started up again. I pulled her closer again and soothed her and stroked her hair.

'When was this, love?' I asked her. 'What did she say to you to make you think that? 'If you can just tell me a little about –'

But she was shaking her head again. 'You can't do anything, Miss. No one can. I just wanted to *tell*. I'm not a liar, Miss, I'm *not*!' she finished, once again animated.

'I know that,' I soothed. 'We *all* know that, Imogen.'

'Gavin doesn't!' she retorted, with shades of the strong voice I'd heard only twice.

'Gavin?'

'He's the liar, Miss!'

'Shhh,' I soothed. 'Shhh … What's Gavin said to you, Imogen? Did he call you a liar? Was that why you got so upset?'

She nodded, rubbing furiously at her eyes again. 'He said I just pretended. But I don't, Miss!'

'Pretended what, Imogen?'

'That I couldn't speak. Just so's you and Miss Vickers would like me the best. So I get more attention. But it's not *true*! He's just an idiot. I don't *want* any attention! I just want to be left alone!' she said, sighing again, heavily. 'They just don't know … They just *don't*, Miss. How can they?' She looked up and at me. 'Sometimes, it's just, like, like when you can't swallow something. It's like I can't even work out how to make it work *myself*.'

I studied her, thinking furiously about how best to play it. Should I go back to Gerri? Ask her more? Try and coax more out of her? Get to the bottom of whatever it was that had happened between them? Something told me no. Something told me I must wait.

'You know the thing with Gavin,' I said instead. 'You know how over-excited he gets sometimes? You know how sometimes he starts getting on everyone's nerves, with his shouting, and his endless chattering, and him running around so much? Well, it's a bit like that for him – sort of like you've just described to me, but in reverse. There's no excuse for anyone calling anyone a liar – of course there isn't – but, like you, sometimes Gavin can't stop himself being, well' – I grinned at her – 'a little bit *too* Gavin-y, just like you struggle to make yourself talk. Do you get that?' Imogen nodded, and I could see she'd absorbed it. 'And today, in particular, well, he was having a bit of a hyper-Gavin day. And then he gets frustrated – just like you do, sometimes – and then he lashes out. And, because you two can't communicate, he doesn't know how hard things are for you. So perhaps that's why he said what he did, and –'

'And he took my book off me as well, Miss.'

159

'And *why* he took your book off you as well. Perhaps just to goad you into saying something to him. Do you think it might be that?'

She nodded again. 'But then he tore it, Miss!' And remembering this made her eyes begin swimming with yet more tears. How much had this child cried? How much did this child *still* cry? Way too much, was my guess. 'Hang on, there,' I said.

I went and grabbed my satchel, opening it as I returned to the computer desk. 'Look,' I said, pulling the loose sheets of her book out. 'Rescued! And here's the book, as well,' I added, handing it to her also. 'And you know what we can do, right this very minute? We can borrow some of Mr Clark's sticky tape and fix it. How about that? And once we've done that, how about we get back to our classroom before the bell goes, and you, me and Gavin can sit down and have a chat about the importance of getting to know each other better?'

Imogen nodded and began putting the torn pages back into order, while I went to Gary's desk and located a roll of Sellotape.

'And I tell you what, Imogen,' I said, 'I have even better news than that. Keep this to yourself – this will just be between you, me and Gavin, okay? – but I have a packet of posh chocolate biscuits as well.'

And an awful lot to start chewing over.

Gavin, predictably, was waiting for the order from the king that he was to be executed by firing squad, at dawn, without trial. Well, that was my guess, based on the expression on his face when Imogen and I returned to the Unit. Kelly was just overseeing an orderly exit for break when we got there, and, seeing us, pulled him back from scooting out.

'Not so fast, mister,' I said, re-routing him back into the classroom. 'I think you and Imogen and I need to have a little chat first. You'll still get your break' – heaven knew, Gavin needed his break time, just to burn off a bit of energy – 'but first we're going to sit down and say some sorrys.'

Gavin slumped in his seat and laid his palms on the table, as if manoeuvring his way around a particularly tricky police interrogation. 'Miss, I am sorry. I'm already sorry. Honest to God, Miss, I'm sorry. I swear on my mother's life – I'll swear on me baby cousin's life, too, if you like – *that's* how sorry I am, Imogen, see?'

I tried very hard not to laugh, and it was something of an achievement that I didn't, but I kept it together sufficiently that I could deliver a short but important lecture about the importance of seeing other people's points of view. It was mainly directed at Gavin, of course, but it didn't hurt to include Imogen in it; she might not be any sort of pest in the classroom, but she was – currently partly of necessity – an introspective only child and it was important she understood that Gavin struggled with challenges too.

But the important thing now, I thought, as I gave them both a biscuit and sent them out to join the others, was to find out exactly what kind of challenges Imogen was struggling with herself. Because an accusation that an adult had been threatening to set fire to her had certainly lit a fire under me.

# Chapter 15

It was to be the following morning before I could get back to Gary and fill him in on my chat with Imogen. I had hoped that I'd be able to catch him during final period, but, as if to remind me that I had more than one child to take care of – and perhaps because they wanted a piece of the action – Henry and Ben kicked off almost as soon as they came back from last break, over some disagreement over the latest Manchester United line-up.

As ever, the full-on fist-fight that honour seemed to dictate must ensue was not really about player stats at all. It was about them – Ben and Henry – two volatile boys always just half a step away from losing the plot. They didn't know it (well, actually, they did, when they were getting on) but they actually had quite a lot in common. For all that Ben was an only child looked after by his heavily drinking dad, and Henry the youngest of five, looked after by his invariably fraught mother, they both brought the same issues to school with them. Both were angry and unable to express it when they were at home – Ben because he always had to be mindful of his father's temper, and Henry because, being the designated 'runt' of the litter, he wasn't allowed to express himself, ever.

I would lie awake at night worrying about children like Henry and Ben, and what if anything I could do to make things better. I couldn't find a new mother for Ben, or make his father quit the drinking, and I couldn't whistle up a father figure for poor put-upon Henry, to lick his bullying, ill-disciplined brothers into shape. In short, I couldn't change their world for them. All I could do – and this always felt like one of the best wisdoms I'd been lucky enough to learn – was to make them change the way they felt about themselves, which would, in turn, change how they interacted *with* their world.

In short, it was all about self-esteem-building, as well as team-building, though in the short term it was also about managing the inevitable flash points that were bound to occur when such boys came into conflict. Fortunately, in this case, it was short lived and easily remedied, with the application of some fact checking, courtesy of my trusty computers, and another round of posh chocolate biscuits.

But that still left me too late to nip up to Gary's office and, not wishing to keep him, given I knew he was taking on a zillion extra duties currently, I decided that the morning would have to do.

Early morning, mind. I was still on something of a mission, so I made a point of getting into school half an hour earlier than usual so that we could talk before registration. I knew sod's law would probably mean I'd get scant opportunity later, and I was also conscious of sticking around, as much as possible, in class. What with Gavin and Imogen, then Ben and Henry, who knew what could happen? Would Shona and Molly launch into fisticuffs next?

Happily, Gary was in and up for chatting, and even managed to rustle me up a coffee, while I nabbed the comfiest of the comfy chairs by his desk.

'So,' he said, settling into his own chair, 'what news on yesterday's cryptic message?'

'Well,' I began, 'if you cast your mind back, you'll remember that I went to visit the step-mother, didn't I? And it turns out the two are related.'

'Of course. The wicked step-mother. I'd forgotten you'd already been round there. How did that go in the end? Get anything of any use?'

'Well, as it happens,' I chided, 'that quip won't seem so funny when I tell you what happened in here after you left yesterday.'

I filled Gary in on what Imogen had told me about her message and how it confirmed what I'd already begun to suspect – that it wasn't the mother but the stepmother who was the mother figure in question – and that could be the root cause I'd been trying to unearth.

'Set light to her, though?' Gary grimaced. 'Sounds a little bit extreme, doesn't it? Slight case of amateur dramatics?'

I shook my head. 'Don't forget, Imogen said she didn't actually do it – but she did threaten it. Pretty frightening in itself. I just wish I could have got some more out of her –

you know, the whys and wherefores, such as when did this happen. But, you know, it just fits. I know I shouldn't be jumping to conclusions, but neither do I want to ignore my gut feeling, having met her. Yes, she came across as the traumatised, oh-so-concerned parent, who only wants the best for Imogen, yadda yadda yadda … but I just don't buy it. There's just something not quite right about her at all.'

'What, like it's an act?'

I shrugged. 'I don't know. She didn't come across as false, not really. But the whole business of there not being any photographs of Imogen. If she was playing some clever game, she'd have slung a few around for effect, wouldn't she? But she obviously isn't that clever. I don't know,' I said again. 'It was just odd. The whole meeting – just odd.'

'But did you learn anything? Find out any more about our silent child's background?'

'Not really. According to Gerri, it was exactly how Mrs Hinchcliffe's always told us. That mummy dearest was apparently a "money-grabbing bitch", with no time for either husband or daughter, and rode out of Dodge with the first man who had more to offer. Then, when Gerri came along, it was a textbook scenario: spoilt only daughter, used to it just being her and Dad, resents the fact that said Dad has now found love with another woman. That's how she told it, at any rate.'

'Hmm,' Gary said, 'bit of an over-reaction, though, wouldn't you say? Resentment is one thing, but mutism in a child of her age? My understanding – if I read Mr Gregory right, anyway – was that you'd expect there to be an episode of real trauma.'

'Which takes me back to what she said about the threat of burning. And I agree – I've read much more now, and from what I've seen of Imogen I just feel we need to take things further. Speak to her dad, at the very least. He's like the Scarlet Pimpernel in all this, isn't he?'

'Disguised as a bit of a doormat, if we're to believe his PR.'

'But you agree with me?'

Gary nodded. 'I agree with you. But Mike's away till after half-term now, so it won't be happening imminently.'

I had forgotten that the head teacher wasn't going to be back till after the holiday. Something to do with budgets – it was invariably something to do with budgets. 'Could we share our concerns with Don then?'

Gary nodded again. 'Yes, we could. But I doubt it'll make much difference, and, anyway, this isn't life or death pressing. She's safe with her grandparents, so she's not in a situation of jeopardy, is she? And I'd rather wait and speak to Mike – formulate a considered plan of action, than start making waves that might forewarn this wicked stepmother of yours. And, to be honest, it'll give you a chance to get a bit more out of Imogen – which, as we don't have a great deal to go on, can't hurt, can it? After all, if we're going to make an allegation of abuse, we're talking social workers, police, the whole kit and caboodle. So we need to be able to back up what we say.' He drained his coffee. The man had a mouth made of asbestos. Which thought, given the situation, certainly felt apt.

* * *

Despite feeling I had Gary on board, I still returned to my classroom feeling disappointed. He was right, of course: Imogen clearly was safe with her grandparents, and perhaps that was part of some grand master plan anyway. The more I thought about it, the more it seemed perfectly plausible that Gerri, ostensibly so nice and so concerned, actually just wanted her new husband's daughter out of the way.

But you couldn't un-think bad thoughts and worrying disclosures. And it seemed to me that it was doubly important I try and get Imogen to tell me more – because if it was an unsubstantiated accusation it could very easily be deflected, and, more and more, my hunch was that she was telling the absolute truth; just the fact of how hard it had been for her to share what she had shared seemed to make it feel all the more likely.

But how to get her talking? As in *really* talking? That was the problem. And one that preoccupied me as I unlocked the door to my room, to find an icy blast whistling through it. I looked up – someone had left one of the top windows open. Probably the caretaker, for reasons I didn't know. It needed shutting, however, because the weather had definitely taken on a wintry feel, so I climbed up onto an art unit and banged it shut again. As I did so, I heard a telltale rustle of paper, and turned around to see the rocket picture the kids had done a couple of weeks back had fallen to the floor, probably as a result of the sudden gust of air-flow. I climbed down and picked it up, and as I pinned it back to the wall I read some of the words on it – all the bad words we'd written and 'sent' off to space. All the bad words we didn't want – and that's when it hit me. My secrets box – why hadn't I thought of that before?

Excited, I went round to my desk and squatted down behind it, rummaging through the top shelf – the place I last recalled seeing it. And that was where it was, too – I was nothing if not obsessively organised – a little scuffed in places, but perfectly serviceable as a postbox.

Which was what it was, being a cylinder of cardboard, painted red, with a slot in the side in which secrets could be posted. It was one of the first tools I'd used when I'd started the Unit. Back then, whenever a new child joined us, out it would come, as well as after every school holiday. I would always explain to the kids that, though it wasn't healthy to carry secrets around with us, sometimes we were in situations when we had no choice. I'd then explain that sometimes sharing a secret might make us feel better about it, even if it was something really scary. I'd then given them the choice, if they had something to get off their chests, to share the secret by writing it down and posting it anonymously, in my box.

The deal was simple. I would read them and, depending on what they wanted, take action or just keep their secret safe with me. They also had the option of adding a name, if they wanted me to know who they were, and, if they felt they'd like to share it in person they could add that, and we could talk, confidentially.

It had been a while since I'd had the box out, which was the sort of thing that sometimes happened. Life was busy, and new strategies and ideas were always circulating, and it had been ages since I'd even given it any thought. And now

I did, I remember there was another aspect to it – there'd been times when it would be routinely filled not so much with important secrets but with tittle-tattle – tale-telling like *Jordan was smoking in the toilets*, or *I heard Mr Moore say 'damn' after assembly*.

But today my box was going to be reinstated for a while, as for a child who had difficulty expressing her secrets via talking this was surely the perfect opportunity to write them down instead. And if it didn't work – she might have decided she had shared too much already, anyway, mightn't she? – well, I hadn't lost anything, after all.

I got the children on the case right away, explaining that as we'd soon be breaking up for half-term it would be a good opportunity to share anything that was worrying them, rather than it festering away over the holidays. I tried not to focus my gaze on Imogen at any point, just had them gather paper and pens while I explained the principles for those who didn't know them, which was most of them, and told them that while they were doing that I would sort out the materials for the morning's activity, which would be to go out into the school grounds on a nature trail cum treasure hunt, looking for leaves and twigs and pine cones and anything else that looked interesting, in order to decorate the classroom for a late autumn display.

It was a popular choice of activity, and the day was perfect for it – bright and cold – and my news set the tone for what I hoped would be a less stressful day than previously. I was also pleased to see that everyone seemed keen to post something, Imogen very much included. Like the others, she had her head down and started scribbling away furiously, writing so much that when the time came to actually post what they'd written, she was the last of the children to come up. I feigned indifference as she posted her piece of paper in the box, folded into a tight, intriguing square. Would this be what we needed? I couldn't wait to open it.

In the meantime, however, it was time to get outside and romp around the school grounds for a bit. I gave each child a plastic bag and we scoured the whole perimeter for goodies; as well as pine cones and acorns and berry-studded twigs, we were able to gather an impressive amount of conkers from the huge horse chestnut on the far edge of the field. It absorbed them for an hour or so, and then, once I felt we'd gathered enough, surprised them by shouting 'Leaf fight!' I then showered Henry and Molly, who were busy inspecting an empty bird's eggshell they'd found, with an armful of dead leaves.

Within seconds, as I knew it would be, it was war. The kids delighted in throwing leaves at me and all over each other, and I was rather shame-faced as the caretaker stomped past us and tutted, making a mental note to assure him we'd sweep them all up again. And, as ever, we attracted a few disapproving looks from a few adjacent classroom windows, the noise we'd made bringing us to the attention of several teachers.

'Okay, everyone,' I said finally, stopping to catch my breath, 'back inside for hot chocolate and marshmallows!'

Disapproval seemed to go with my job. I knew that my techniques had been the subject of heated classroom debate more than once, one line of thinking being that I was sending the wrong message. Behave yourself in school, so the argument ran, and your reward is simply work. Act like a prat, on the other hand, and look forward to skipping proper lessons and having fun. Most weren't so simplistic – most of the teachers knew these kids and their challenges – but I knew the odd pocket of teachers who seemed to think that. And, actually, they couldn't have been more wrong.

Yes, rewards played a big part in what I did, but that was an essential, because it was all about changing expectations. Most of the kids that were sent to me – particularly those affected by difficult home lives and behavioural issues – couldn't cope long enough in mainstream classes to get rewarded for anything, and came from home environments where rewards were pretty thin on the ground too. Being in the Unit, for many of these children, was a rare opportunity to be in an environment where they could relax and not be constantly expecting the worst. It was a place where they'd be bigged up for the smallest good thing – not as a way of over-inflating their egos (these were children who'd often had their egos comprehensively trampled) but as a way of reintroducing the idea that they could be proud of themselves and that praise and reward were good feelings. It was all about breaking the cycle of feeling useless, acting in accordance with low expectations, getting punished and having your low opinion of yourself confirmed.

It was also about having fun, and I remained unrepentant. Maybe one day I'd deliver a serious lecture on the business of why fun, as a concept for kids like these, mattered.

But perhaps not today. Today I had other more pressing matters to attend to, and as the bell went for break I couldn't wait for the room to clear, so I could get my hands on my little postbox full of notes.

And I wasn't to be disappointed.

The first was intriguing.

I am going to see a speshalist doctor cos my mum thinks I'm mental. Don't tell the other kids, will you.
Gavin.

I smiled and put it to one side. For all his eccentricities, Gavin certainly wasn't 'mental'. Did his mother think he was? I didn't think so. He had obviously been referred, though. I wondered what for.

I smacked my little cousin and I feel bad.

This one was unsigned, but I felt sure it was from Shona. She'd written in neat capitals, presumably in an attempt to disguise her writing, but I knew that in the great scheme of things it would be worth bringing up, so that she had the opportunity of talking it through, albeit couched in more general terms.

Robert Small called me a sad sack – Molly.

Poor Molly. Although she'd started speaking up for herself a bit more, Molly attracted bullies like a flame attracted moths. I made another mental note – time for another of our regular chats about finding ways to better stand up for yourself.

The next one I picked up was definitely from Imogen – I remembered how many times she'd folded it. And, instinctively, I put it to one side for the moment, while I read the two remaining bits of paper.

The next was blank. Which was odd, as I'd seen everybody writing. Another mental note – to think about that later. And the next made me start, as well as smile:

I fancy Imogen.

Well, well, I thought, trying to work out who had written it, narrowing it down logically to either Henry or Ben, which meant it had to be Ben. With him being that bit younger, perhaps he had a bit of a crush on her, despite him always following Henry's lead and ribbing her. That was often the way when it came to boys. Ribbing the object of their burgeoning attraction was one of the surest ways of getting their attention. I smiled to myself and added it to the pile.

And now I was back to Imogen's herself; the prompt to get the box out in the first place. Would she finally find the wherewithal to share a little more? I unfolded the sheet of A4, not quite daring to hope, but immediately realising there was a great deal written on it, which took the form of a neatly penned list.

Gerri used to lock me in my room while she went to the cat shows.

Gerri told my dad I wet my bed when she wouldn't let
    me go to the toilet. She locked me up.
Gerri told me my mum left us because I'm ugly like
    my dad and have gingery hair.
Gerri didn't give me any food when dad worked away
    and she said she'd hit me if I told him.
Gerri pulled my hair and said she would cut it all off
    when I went to sleep.
She cried to my nan and said I tried to push her down
    the steps cos I hated her and my nan believed her.
She told my dad I stole money from her purse and
    that I let her cats out on purpose.
I thought she was going to set fire to me.

I set the letter down and returned the rest to the postbox, which I then returned to the back of the shelf under my desk. I then picked up the letter again, grabbed my satchel, left the classroom and locked it, before hurrying to the staffroom to see if Kelly was in there, as I needed her to come hold the fort after break so I could track Gary down.

I had what I needed. The head would surely have to take this seriously.

# Chapter 16

They say a week is a long time in politics. By which I think they mean that an awful lot can change in a few days, what with politics being such a volatile business. A week is also a long time when you're privy to what amounts to some pretty shocking allegations and can do absolutely nothing about them.

Gary had agreed with me, of course, that Imogen's allegations about her stepmother were, indeed, shocking, but with the headmaster away and half-term imminent he was still of the opinion that we should sit on what we knew till his return.

'Nothing's changed,' he said. 'This is great – grim but great, assuming it's true –'

'Gary, trust me. I believe her *completely*.'

'I trust your judgement, don't worry. But we still need to run it by Mike. There are protocols that need to be followed here, before we go to social services, and, as she's safe with her grandparents, which we know she currently is, let's all

175

enjoy our break and make this a priority as soon as we're back, okay?'

Which had to be okay, since there was little I could do about it. But, while I understood the reasoning and, for the greater part, agreed with it, there was still a part of me that refused to stop fretting. In fact, to say I spent half-term 'preoccupied' was something of an understatement, and rattling round an empty house – Mike and Riley at work, Kieron busy in college – didn't help a jot.

Suppose I'd tipped Gerri off in some way, just by visiting? Suppose she was scared now – which would be good, no doubt about it, a taste of her own medicine – but suppose she started taking it out on Imogen? Supposing she was threatening her again, even now, with all sorts of horrible punishments, if she told the social workers what she'd told me in her note? Supposing I had opened a can of worms even wrigglier than the proverbial? Supposing bad things happened as a result?

Needless to say, I was in school bright and early the following Monday and all but ran to Gary's office to see if there was any news.

'News?' he guffawed. 'Blimey, Casey, are you on something or what? I've barely got my coat off!'

But he was mostly teasing, because he had actually already been in school for half an hour, and had already put a note on the headmaster's desk asking if he could speak to him as a matter of urgency about a child-protection issue.

Which mollified me somewhat, though I was also a realist, and one thing I realised was that Mike Moore would have returned to an overflowing in-tray, and had well over 1,000 pupils to worry about, not just one. So we'd have to wait our turn, but I hoped we wouldn't be on tenterhooks for too long, as, whatever else was going on, a child had disclosed that she'd been the victim of abuse in the not too distant past, which made it a matter of some urgency in anybody's language.

'Okay, Gary,' I said, 'but you will tell me the very minute you hear anything, won't you? I'll have Kelly on standby so I'll be able to come up at a moment's notice.'

Gary laughed his usual laid-back laugh. Perhaps keeping your cool was a prerequisite to doing the sort of full-on job that he did. 'Don't worry, Casey,' he said. 'I know what you're like. I'll have my carrier pigeon good to fly soon as I get word.'

The children were all like bottles of pop, which was fairly standard in the Unit after any sort of break. Fairly standard for school generally, as everyone caught up on everyone else's important news, which was obviously much too important to be derailed by boring stuff like keeping silent during registration, something that regularly challenged at least two of my kids in any case.

So I eased them in gently. 'Ten minutes chatting time,' I told them, 'and then we get started, okay?' Then began getting prepared for our first period, which would mostly be involving poetry.

Poetry was one of my staples at this time of year. Lock some of these children in a room with a pen and a sheet of paper with the instruction to 'write a poem' and from their reaction you might expect to be arrested for committing war crimes, such was the sense of cold dread it could invoke. But give them a trigger – particularly one with lots of meaty imagery and connotations – and you could, if you were gentle, coax all manner of surprising word-combinations from them.

We'd just had Halloween – plenty of meaty imagery and connotations there, for starters – and as the last half-term had fallen close to 5 November there had been lots of organised firework displays already. So there was something for everyone: dead souls and ghouls, clanking chains, and trick-or-treating or pyrotechnics, loud bangs and burnings at the stake.

I began handing out workbooks and pens and coloured pencils, and as I did so I noticed that Imogen had taken herself off to the far side of the girls' table, while the other five were all currently gathered around the boys' one. What was her news, I wondered? Whatever it was, she obviously wasn't keen to share it. No, she wouldn't have much to say, I knew, but she'd normally at least be there, close beside Shona, taking her cues from her friend.

'Imogen, love,' I said quietly, not wanting to make a big deal of it and start stressing her. 'Why don't you join the others at the boys' table for a bit. Like I said, we're not starting straight away.'

She'd had her head bowed, nose in book, as was standard, but now she looked up at me and I was shocked by just how wretched she appeared. Her face was pale and puffy. She'd clearly been doing a lot of crying. She shook her head by way of an answer and returned to scanning the pages.

I leaned down. 'You okay, sweetie?' I whispered. She shook her head, but, again, didn't say anything. Not even in the monosyllabic way she'd become used to doing in class now. Oh God, I thought, had she slipped back to her mutism again? In so many other areas, kids did tend to slip back a little when out of school – and in this too? And what was the cause? Was it simply the week at home? The heightened anxiety about returning after the break? Or was it because of something more sinister?

I squatted beside her. 'Imogen, love,' I whispered, 'I'm going to come straight to the point, okay? Have you stopped speaking again?'

I watched and waited and, presumably with no place to go, she eventually raised her gaze and met mine. Then she nodded, and as she did so I heard the door open behind me. It was Kelly. And, seeing her, Imogen immediately shrank back and lowered her head again.

Damn, I thought, standing up. This was a setback. And perhaps it wasn't just about half-term; maybe it was because she'd been thinking. Maybe she'd been worrying that she'd said too much in her 'secrets' note to me, and would now be in trouble. But whatever it was, there was no way I'd find out at this moment. I went back to join Kelly – who I still needed to bring up to speed – and get the day under way.

'Right then,' I began, once I'd had the kids return to their usual working places, 'from what I've just heard, it sounds like you're all going to have lots to write about this morning. Not in the shape of a story, however. Today I'm after two pieces of poetry.' There was the usual groan from

179

the boys – something that seemed almost automatic – but I was used to that, so I carried straight on. 'The first,' I told them, 'I want to be all about Halloween. Any aspect of it: how much you enjoyed it, which parts of it scared you, what you might have dressed up as; and the second piece I want to be about Guy Fawkes Night, which I know hasn't happened yet, but did any of you go and see any fireworks over the weekend? Have bonfires? Make a guy, or …'

I stopped in mid-sentence, because Imogen, previously just sitting there, head bent, had jumped from her chair, which fell back and landed with a clatter, made a dash for the door and ran from the room.

The other kids stared, open mouthed, just as I did. 'Imogen?' I called. But it was too late. She'd gone. 'Okay, everyone,' I said, to forestall another wave of chatter. 'You know what you're doing now. Any questions, ask Miss Vickers, while I go and find Imogen, but come on, chop-chop, let's get those thinking caps on, okay?'

I left the classroom, then, expecting to have to start stalking the corridors, but Imogen hadn't gone very far at all. I fact, she was sitting cross-legged on the floor, back against the wall. Just by the door. I squatted down beside her and laid a hand on her shoulder. 'Sweetie, what's the matter?' I asked her, as the tears started up. 'Something's clearly wrong but if you don't tell me what it is I can't help you, can I? Come on, *try*,' I coaxed, which only made her cry harder. My instinct was obviously to gather her into my arms but I stopped myself. I needed not to provide a method of retreat but to keep her outside her comfort zone, so I actually moved away slightly, then stood up, then extended my hand.

'Come on, sweetie,' I said, gesturing towards it. 'Come on, let's go somewhere more private. Somewhere quiet where you can tell me what's wrong.'

It took a while but eventually she slipped her hand into mine, and once I had a hold of her I helped to pull her up. 'Good girl,' I said, as we headed off down the corridor. 'Now let's go and see if Mr Clark's office is free.'

And, thankfully, it was. Perhaps he was even then deep in conversation with the head. Perhaps he wasn't, but either way I knew he wouldn't mind us taking refuge in his room. There was a box of tissues on his windowsill and, seeing it, I grabbed a handful. 'Here, love,' I said to Imogen, 'now have a blow and wipe your eyes and then you can tell me what's upsetting you, okay?'

She duly took the tissues and blew her nose, but it was like stopping a leaky dam. She was still crying and I suspected she would continue to do so, until such time as she got this huge weight off her chest. But the speaking bit – that was probably going to be the hard part.

'Imogen,' I said, taking a seat opposite her, 'I know this is going to be difficult, now you've gone to that place in your head, but, honestly, it's just a question of starting. If you can just get the first few words out, the rest will be easy, so let's start at the beginning and get the hardest part over with. Now, before half-term you put your secret letter in my box and you knew I was going to read it – is that what's upsetting you?'

Again I waited, resisting the urge to fill the lengthening silence, while Imogen again blew her nose and dabbed at the tears on her cheeks. 'No, Miss,' she said finally. 'It's not that.'

'Well done,' I said. 'There. That's a start, isn't it? Okay, so it's not that, so has something bad happened?'

She twisted the life out of another bunch of tissues before answering. 'It was our Bonfire Night, Miss,' she said. 'My nan and grandad did a party, for a surprise.'

'A firework party?' I prompted.

She nodded. 'An' they never told me. And they invited my dad to come. And *her*.'

Now we were getting somewhere. And that was interesting. Were they trying to build bridges? Help effect a reconciliation? Take the school's lead and try to get Imogen back home? How ironic. 'Gerri?' I asked gently. 'Your step-mum?'

She nodded. But didn't speak. So now I did prompt her. 'And what happened, love?' I asked her. 'Did she *do* something? Hurt you again?'

She shook her head decisively. Wrong track, then. 'It was the fire,' she said. 'And her being there. And the way she kept *grinning* at me. Miss, she's *horrible*! And I knew why she was grinning at me, too. She was doing it to remind me. About how she could set fire to me too.'

She was getting into her stride now, fear and anger helping her to overcome her difficulties. And it was important things stay that way too.

'Imogen, you know what you told me about how you thought Gerri was going to set fire to you? Do you think you could tell me what you meant? What actually happened? What made you think that would happen?'

And as she started to tell me, I realised that what I'd said to her was true, because once she began, out it came, like a flood.

'My dad was away working in Italy,' she said, 'and was going to be away for two days. And we'd been arguing, like we always did, and she'd refused to let me have anything to eat. And when I went into my room, she locked it – all the rooms in my dad's house have keys because of valuables –'

'Valuables?'

'Because my dad works away lots.'

'Ah, okay.'

'Anyway, she said I could stay there till I stopped being horrible and I told her I'd scream out the window so the neighbours could hear me and she told me she'd tell them I was horrible and naughty and that I screamed to get attention, because that's what she always said she'd say if I told her I'd tell on her. So I told her I'd kick the door in and tell my dad, but she didn't take any notice, and in the end, after hours and hours, I must have fell asleep. And then when I woke up it was really dark – it was night-time by now, I think, and I woke up and I was wet and I could smell something funny and at first I thought I must have peed the bed. I'd never done that, not since I was really, really little, but I was warm and wet and then I saw her, sitting in my chair. Which was really frightening, and when I sat up she told me I'd better not move too much because I might go up in flames. I didn't really know what she was on about at first, but then she showed me. She had my dad's petrol can

– you know those green plastic ones you get in petrol stations? One of those. And she had this lighter. And she kept flicking the flame on in front of me, and she told me I was wet because she'd soaked me in dad's emergency petrol and that she'd woken me up so that I would have a chance to say a prayer before she burned me to death.'

To say I couldn't believe what I was hearing was wrong, because, for reasons that had no basis in evidence, I *did* believe it. But, even so, a part of me still *couldn't* believe it – how could anyone inflict such cruelty on a child?

In years to come I would have that question answered, and comprehensively, but right then I asked the question that seemed the only one *to* ask. 'Love,' I said gently, 'did this actually happen? This wasn't just part of some horrible dream?'

'Yes, Miss!' she said immediately. 'I mean she didn't actually burn me. And it wasn't even petrol. She'd just poured water over me. That's why I thought I'd peed, because it was warm, but she told me it was petrol. And I could smell it. She'd put some on a hankie, so I could smell it …'

'I'm sorry, love,' I rushed to reassure her. 'Of course I believe you. So what happened next?'

'I was terrified. She kept flicking the lighter on and off. So I begged her not to burn me and she started laughing and telling me I was pathetic and telling me I had to beg some more. I had to say, *Please, I'm so ugly, but please don't set fire to me*, and she kept doing that for ages and then burst out laughing again and telling me it was all a big joke. That's when she told me about the water and said how silly

I was for believing it, and said that if I told dad she really *would* burn me, and that it was just to show me how she would do it if she had to. That now I knew just how easy it would be, and that I should be very careful not to annoy her.'

Which was when a half-remembered thought suddenly came to me. What had the woman said to me that day, about winning all those trophies? That was it. That it was *all about attention to the little details*.

I took Imogen into my arms then and tried to soothe her racking sobs. No wonder she'd been stunned into silence, I thought. She must have been scared half to death by such wickedness.

*Attention to detail. How easy it would be.* This was a monster, and I was speechless myself.

# Chapter 17

With Kelly already looking after my kids, I used the internal phone to call Jim Dawson, and while we waited for him to arrive I impressed upon Imogen that she was not in any trouble whatsoever. And that, actually, what she'd done had been very brave and very important and that once her nan and grandad knew (I was careful not to mention her father) they would make sure she was safe.

This had brought on another intense bout of sobbing as she revealed that her nan had given her a huge telling off for stomping off to her bedroom and spoiling their party, and how fed up they were getting of her living there.

Which made me wince, but, of course, that was exactly what would happen, her wicked stepmother having done such a brilliant job of painting this child – who she clearly hated, for whatever twisted reason – as some spoilt and odious kid set on trouble.

But it was trouble that was about to be heaped on her

own head, and, boy, I thought, as I sped off to track Gary Clark down, would I *love* to see that happen.

Just as I'd hoped, Gary was indeed in a meeting with the head, and, hopefully, as a part of his doubtless long list of items, discussing the action the school should now take. And as the receptionist confirmed that there were only the two of them in there, I had little hesitation, despite the *Meeting in progress* sign hanging on it, in rapping sharply on the door.

'I'm sorry to interrupt,' I said, as both men looked up at me in surprise, 'but there's been something of a development with Imogen Hinchcliffe.'

Gary gave me a 'What the hell?' look as Jim stood to greet me. 'Come on in, Casey. How are you? Rested after half-term, I hope? Come and grab a chair, and let's hear what you've got for us. Gary's already filled me in on where we're at with her written disclosures, but you've something else now?'

'I have,' I said. 'She's been talking to me. Properly talking,' I added. 'About the first thing she told us.' I glanced at Gary. 'About thinking her stepmother was going to burn her? Well, now she's told me the full circumstances and it's shocking, it really is.'

'Which are?' Gary asked.

So I told them. Both men listened in the same shocked silence that I had, and when I'd finished Mike Moore spread his hands. 'I'm at a loss for words,' he said. 'And I'm not trying to be funny. Where's she now?'

'In Gary's office with Jim Dawson, currently,' I told him. 'In no fit state to stay in school but, well, where do we go now? Can we really just send her home, now, to nan and grandad, business as usual?'

He turned to Gary. 'As CPO, what are your thoughts?' he asked him. 'What's the next step we should take at this point?'

'Well,' said Gary, 'it's both complicated and made easier by the fact that she's already living with her grandparents. Complicated because it makes intervention more complex as there is another layer of family involved, but easier in that, as far as we know, she's already in a place of safety, so there will hopefully be no need for an emergency intervention – picking her up and placing her in care; that sort of thing.'

'Well, that's something,' I agreed, thinking just what a trauma it would be for Imogen to be taken away and placed in the care of strangers. The implications for her mutism could be potentially catastrophic. 'So what *would* happen?'

'Well, the key thing is probably the dad here. We've yet to speak to him, so we don't yet know what part he's played. On the face of it, all this has been going on in his absence, and, from what Imogen herself says, without his knowledge.'

Mike tutted, and I knew exactly what he was wondering: just how foolish or, indeed, hands-off a parent had to be not to see what was happening right underneath their nose. But it was unfair to prejudge him, I supposed, not without getting all the facts. 'And what a shock he's going to get,' I said.

Gary shook his head. 'Not necessarily. Odds are he is, but there are lots of abuse cases where the uninvolved parent has known what's going on – in some cases, exactly what's been going on – but, for whatever reason, has chosen to ignore it. Sometimes it's coercion, or fear of retaliation, but sometimes it's just plain expediency. And after all, this is a man who's been left with his daughter, but who has a job that means he has to work away. It could well be that he's chosen to turn a bind eye on how she's been treating his daughter because he needs her to take on the lion's share of the childcare. Trust me, people can talk themselves into all sorts of things – it's just a case of skimming over the details and shutting your ears a tiny bit. No,' he said finally, 'this is a complex situation. And, happily, it's not our job to sort it out.'

He stood up then. 'So, assuming you are okay with it, Mike, I'm off to bend some ears at social services. They'll decide how to proceed from there, and I imagine it will involve the police, but in the meantime you need to get this all written up, Casey. So I'll pop down and see Kelly, make sure she's coping okay with your lot, then I'll make the call. Okay to tell them you'll email a full report to them shortly?'

I nodded. 'So what happens to Imogen? Like, right now I mean. She's still in your office.'

'Ah, yes,' he said. 'And it probably wouldn't be sensible to take her back to the Unit, so maybe you could sort out some work for her to be getting on with till we know what's happening? We could have her go down to learning support – I'm sure Julia Styles will be happy to take care of her. Yes, that'll work best for the moment, don't you think?'

I told him it would, and that I'd have someone fetch her

bag up and her reading book. I suspected that the last thing she'd want to do currently was pen poetry about fireworks and bonfires. She'd had enough of the latter for the fore-seeable future, and as for the fireworks – well, they were just about to start.

It took less than an hour for the business of child protec-tion to lumber into action. It was just before lunch when, my report finally written, I'd headed to Gary's office so I could email it to the contact at social services. And now we were under way, Gary hadn't let the grass grow.

'I've already spoken to the grandparents,' he told me, once I'd forwarded the email. 'And put them in the picture. And the social worker will be in touch with them, too. In the meantime, grandad's going to pick Imogen up at lunch-time, as there's no point in her being here this afternoon, not in the state she's in. The key thing is going to be convincing her that she's not in any trouble, and the grand-parents are aware of that as well – as they are about the fact that it's essential that they don't speak to either their son or their daughter-in-law until social services have been in touch and the authorities have done their bit.'

'What an awful situation,' I said.

'Tell me about it. The grandmother's devastated. Can't quite take it in, as you'd expect.'

'And must feel awful, too,' I said. 'Must feel so guilty about not believing her. And all this time … God, that poor, poor kid.'

'But it's over now, all being well,' Gary said briskly. And I didn't doubt that he'd see that it was so.

'So what *is* going to happen next?' I asked him. 'What's the course of events now it's with social services? Will they go round and visit the house? Investigate? Bring them in to their offices and interview them?'

Gary gave me a look that was part way between a smile and a smirk.

'Nothing so polite,' he said. 'That tends not to be how it works.'

'How does it work then?'

'They will simply have the police go and arrest them.'

I returned to the Unit after lunch with my head full of horrible images but my hands no longer full – not where Imogen was concerned, anyway – and it was a decidedly odd feeling. It was absolutely the way of things in my job – children came to you, you did what you could, then they left you; that was the job. And, actually, chances were that nothing much would change.

Gary's pronouncement had really brought it home to me, no doubt about it. And the picture I'd subsequently painted – complete with sirens, reading of rights and trophy-winning cat fanciers being handcuffed and thrown into the backs of police riot vans, and into cages – was undeniably a pleasing one, and no less than she deserved. But, in the midst of all that, Imogen would still need to go to school. Yes, the grandparents could keep her home, I guessed, and no one would castigate them for doing so, but as she was already removed from the situation there wasn't any clear and present danger, and my hunch was that every-one would suggest it was in her best interests – particularly re the selective mutism – for it to indeed be a case of business as usual, particularly if it transpired, and I was still confident it would, that her father had not been involved.

But that still left a hole in my brain's Sherlock Holmes region. It was no longer my job to investigate anything. It was now in the hands of the professionals. And, as if to remind me, when I returned to the Unit after lunch break it was to find my attention drawn to the collection of pine cones in the corner, which took my thoughts to Christmas, and, by extension, to Shona, who was sitting with Molly currently, but staring into space.

It was a mental gear change, and an important one, as I had six children to think about, and for one of them, at least, the coming festivities would be incredibly difficult. I was very aware how much time was devoted in school to Christmas – not just to the occasion itself and the opportunities for fostering the children's spiritual education, but to the day-to-day business of planning Christmas-related events, such as the special assemblies, the making and giving of cards, the various decorating sessions, the end-of-term parties and the community activities, such as the school's annual carol service at the local church, for which I had a smidgin of a germ of an idea.

All of this, for Shona, would be torture. And I was also mindful that her 'secret' hinted at a difficult set of circumstances, ones that, in reality, only time could make better.

Which put another small idea into my head. As she'd not known how long I'd be out of the Unit, Kelly – ever the human dynamo – had already organised everything for that afternoon's lessons, which would be maths followed by science.

As Shona's maths was generally sound, bordering on comfortably above average, I decided I would pull her out of the first half of the afternoon, so we'd have some privacy to chat, if she felt so inclined. It would also give me a chance to bring up the secrets box, if it seemed appropriate, though I was mindful that she'd taken pains to keep her secret anonymous, so I'd have to let her take the lead on that.

The inquest into 'Where's Imogen Gone and What Was Wrong with Her?' dealt with (easily attributed to a 24-hour tummy bug), I had a quick word with Kelly, then went over to speak to Shona. As well as being good at maths, she had an impressive artistic talent, which, today, served my needs very well. 'I'm in need of a volunteer,' I explained, 'to help me create a thing of beauty for the display wall in the main reception, and I said to myself, "Who's the undisputed champion of all things creative in the Unit, if not the entire lower school?" And guess which name sprang to mind?'

Shona smiled delightedly, which was gladdening in itself.

'So you're up for it?' I asked.

'I'd *love* to, Miss,' she answered.

'Good,' I said. 'Grab your coat because it's cold in the entrance, and let's go and create a masterpiece, shall we?'

Putting children's work on display was a central part of every teaching job, and though I wasn't strictly speaking a teacher myself – my job title being the slightly more menacing 'Behaviour Manager' – I was still on the rota to provide displays for the boards in all the school's communal areas, and mine was due to replace the current one by the end of that very week.

I'd already partly prepared and decided upon a theme for our display: a perennial and a bit of a classic, autumn colours. I'd squirrelled away various things already – mostly pictures and drawings, and the main 'event' would be the poems they had produced only that morning, which I would have them write out again, in their very best writing, and then decorate around the edges with whatever took their fancy. For now, though, it was a question of preparing the background and, as I suspected, Shona was full of ideas about what might look nice. We'd brought down my big plastic display box – full of all the tools of the trade – and we were soon immersed in choosing borders and materials and possible colours.

'So,' I said, at length, 'how are you getting on, love? Are you still seeing your counsellor?'

Shona nodded. 'She's nice. We go for walks sometimes now. Which is nice ...'

She trailed off, then, and I let the silence lengthen. Then, while manoeuvring a particularly petulant piece of border into position, said, 'I suppose it must be nice to get away from time to time. You know, from your little cousins – have some space for yourself.'

'That's what she said.' She handed me the wall-stapler. 'I'm not that used to it – having so many people around all the time ... all the noise.'

'That's what little ones are best at usually, aren't they?'

She nodded. 'And they want me to play with them all the time. And I try to – I want to be helpful, because I know my auntie's always so busy …'

'But sometimes you just want to scream – go away!'

Her answering smile confirmed I'd hit the nail on the head, as well as the staple into the wall. 'I know what you mean,' I said. 'And with the holidays coming up, you'll have to brace yourself a bit, won't you?'

'I already am,' she said, after a pause of presumably reflection. 'I'm going to miss school – you know, seeing my friends, having stuff to do.'

'You'll be able to see some of them, though, won't you? At some point over the holidays? Sales shopping, catching up, that sort of thing?'

'I guess so,' she said, 'but it's like family time, isn't it?'

I hesitated, sensing from her body language that she didn't want to dwell on that. 'And lots of tedious board games and leftover turkey,' I decided upon. 'Though I have a cunning plan for all that.' I grinned at her. 'And I know I'll need to come in here at some point, so I'll have an official "going to work" day between Christmas and New Year, when I'll come in here, while it's quiet, and get my classroom sorted out. Pull down the old displays, get all inspired, set up the backgrounds for all the new ones. That way, when term starts, I'm ready for action – with my walls set up for all the new term's creations. And have a few hours peace and quiet. Bet it'll work a treat.'

I don't know if it was her expression or just a bolt of inspiration, but an idea pinged on in my head then and there. 'And you know what? I could always use a helper to do that too – what with being such a shortie. So, there's a thought; assuming the head's okay with it, and I telephone your auntie to ask her, would you perhaps like to come in one day and do that with me too?'

Now it was definitely her expression that cemented it. 'Could I?'

'I don't see why not,' I said. 'If it's something you'd like to do.'

'Oh, I'd *love* to, Miss,' she said again.

'Then I'd love that too. And I shall pay you in hot chocolate and pink and white marshmallows. That's the going rate – how does that sound?'

Her giggle warmed my heart for the rest of the day.

# Chapter 18

I woke up the next morning with my head still madly buzz-ing – with the same stuff that had preoccupied me when I'd gone to bed the night before: what was happening with the wicked stepmother, that I needed to speak to the head and to Shona's auntie, whether I should take the plunge and ask if my class could do a turn at the Christmas carol service, whether I should call Gavin's mother and see how things were – try to establish quite why she thought he was 'mental' … And it made me think of something Don had said to me towards the end of my first term in school, after I'd commented on the fact that I kept losing my keys, and seemed to have my head on back to front.

'It's called end-of-term-itis,' he'd pronounced, nodding sagely. 'And it goes with the territory. There's a reason why teachers need the year broken up into terms; as they go on, you find it harder and harder to switch off and clear your mind. Have you found that?'

'Exactly that. Like a kind of burn-out,' I'd said, nodding.

'Though only of a temporary kind, thankfully. Everyone gets it. Couple of weeks to recharge and you'll be set for the new term. You'll see.'

And I *had* seen, and these days I was more in tune with the termly rhythms, but right now, however, we still had four weeks of the current term to go, and, what with all the drama we'd had lately – particularly with Imogen – I profoundly hoped they'd be mostly without incident. A happy, twinkly run-up to Christmas was what I was hoping for, so I sent a quick wish to the elves at the North Pole, hoping Santa would be so kind as to oblige me.

I ran my hands over my face and sat in bed for a few moments longer, listening to the strangely soothing sound of Kieron downstairs, banging pans around while engaged in some sort of breakfast-related mission, and hearing Riley's always dulcet 'I'm-getting-ready-for-work-so-keep-out-of-my-way' tones. It was getting to that time of year: dark in the mornings, even darker in the evenings – but with the joys of Christmas still very slightly over the horizon, however much the shops would have it otherwise. There was just too much work to be done between now and then.

I got out of bed finally and opened the curtains, even if it was only to look out on a still inky darkness. Poor Mike was long gone. Would have been at work for an hour already. The shifts he did were particularly gruelling at this time of year. I glanced back at my bedside clock. I would have to get my skates on as well – there was a big important meeting to attend in school this morning, and before that I really needed to get organised. My mind was still on

Shona, to some extent – I wasn't sure I agreed that she should go back to mainstream classes this side of Christmas – but the main priority today was Imogen and what was going to happen there.

Mostly, I was intrigued about what we'd find out. We'd been told snippets of course, but they were tantalisingly vague ones. That the investigation had turned up some 'interesting' background details, that there'd been talk of various measures that were now going to be 'put in place', but what all of that meant in practice was anyone's guess.

What *had* they found out? And about whom? Gerri, I guessed, but what about Imogen's father? Could he really have been so naïve as to let such horrors go on under his nose? I fervently hoped so, for Imogen's sake.

'Yes,' came the emphatic answer a couple of hours later.

It was a larger gathering than I'd expected. So much so that we'd had to hold it in the conference room in the library, which was usually reserved for training, as we'd have struggled to fit us all into one of the smaller offices.

As well as Gary and myself, present were Jim Dawson (my alter ego), Julia Styles (our Special Needs Co-ordinator, or SENCO) and, as well as Don (standing in for the head, who was at a financial meeting), there were two social workers, a tall man called Simon Swift, who had apparently now been allocated to the family, and a trainee called Helen Croft, who he explained was attached to him currently and who was apparently 'cutting her teeth' on Imogen's case.

The main purpose of the meeting was to bring us up to speed. So the first 20 minutes or so had been spent putting us fully in the picture, from the moment the investigation had been launched by social services, as a consequence of Imogen's disclosures to me and Gary's subsequent call.

And I was all ears, because it was as much an education for me as it was for the trainee social worker. I'd had dealings with social services before this, both in my current job and as a youth worker before that, but this was the first time I'd been so much at the centre of a process that could – and would – have such a profound effect on a child's home life; something that felt like quite a responsibility.

No, it didn't involve taking a child from their home – Imogen was already out of harm's way, because she was staying with her grandparents – but the emotional trauma she had been caused, and was still suffering the effects of, was something that would have continued, one way or another, had she not found the courage to tell me what she had that day.

An intervention had clearly been necessary – and quite a dramatic one, by the sound of it. Choosing their moment, so that both Gerri and Graham Hinchcliffe had been at home, the social workers had gone to the house, accompanied by a police officer, who had done just as Gary had predicted – arrested both husband and wife on suspicion of assault and wilful neglect.

'And, as luck would have it – well, I suppose that's one way of putting it – it turns out that Gerri Hinchcliffe had a previous conviction,' Simon Swift explained, 'and it was for a similar offence. That was a key piece of evidence. And, luckily – well, in terms of the amount of paperwork involved, definitely – she didn't even try to deny it. In fact, she laughed,' he continued, glancing at Gary, to whom he'd obviously already told the tale. 'She said – let me see if I can remember it right – yes, she said, "It was only f***ing water. How could I ever harm her with f***ing water, for f***s sake? You can't do me for her being a gullible little cow!"' He cleared his throat and grinned, then. 'Nice, eh? And, of course, fortunately, yes we can.'

'So Imogen made a statement to you okay, then?' I asked. This had been my major concern, that when it came to it, and faced with having to speak to complete strangers – and in what would feel like very intimidating surroundings, however 'cosy' they made the places where children had to do such things – she would simply clam up and be unable to get anything out. But it seemed I didn't need to worry.

'Indeed she did,' Simon reassured me. 'Which made everything all the more straightforward. Gerri Hinchcliffe has been released on bail, but Imogen's dad was released without charge pretty much straight away, and was able to reassure her that she wasn't in any trouble. He really *didn't* have a clue – that was immediately obvious. And his wife had certainly covered her tracks very well. Anyway, he asked her to leave his house that same day, apparently. Which I believe she has now done. Along with her cats.'

And their many rosettes and trophies, no doubt. I shook my head. 'I can't believe such cruelty,' I said. 'Well, I *can*, obviously. We see it all around us, after all. But to treat a defenceless child like that and *laugh* about it – and to social services? It beggars belief, doesn't it? And to have everyone fooled by her – incredible to think she could take everyone in so convincingly. That's what really gets me. I mean, I've never heard the nan do anything but sing her praises!'

'Not any more,' Gary corrected. 'And the poor woman's really quite traumatised, as you can imagine. As is the grandfather. Because they were completely taken in by her, every bit as much as their son was. Which at least makes his own ignorance a touch more credible, I suppose.'

Simon nodded. 'And it's far from unusual, I'm afraid. If I had a pound for every case I've seen where the guilty party has been able to do something like this entirely under the radar – entirely without anyone suspecting a thing – then I'd be a very rich man indeed, believe me. But we're dealing with someone with profound emotional problems. This is a woman who's something of a narcissist. Someone whose own mother abandoned her at a very young age and has, in the main, been brought up in care – a succession of children's homes, by all accounts. And though, superficially, she's quite charming, and seems to have done okay for herself, this is a woman for whom the word "empathy" might as well be written in Mandarin; someone who uses and abuses as a default. And we all know how it works, I'm sure –' He glanced around the room and he was right. We all knew *exactly* what he was talking about. 'These people are often very charismatic and independent-minded, aren't they? They certainly don't wear a badge saying "avoid at all costs", do they?'

And also shrewd. Imogen's father, cuckolded and left and hurt as he was, would have been an obvious target. Was she holidaying alone on one of his coach trips when she snared him? 'So what will happen to her now?' I asked, managing to feel only marginally less forgiving of her. Though, given her background, I knew I should, I still couldn't forget what she'd done to Imogen.

'She's been charged and she will be prosecuted for cruelty and neglect. And if she doesn't exactly learn the error of her ways, we can at least hope it will deter her from striking up any new relationships with men who have children to consider. We'll obviously let you know how things progress, but as far as Imogen is concerned this period is over and we're going to be working with the family to get her life back on track. And – hopefully – that will feed into progress with her speech therapy.'

I was just about to ask if there was anything in particular that I should or shouldn't be doing with Imogen in the light of recent developments, when the meeting was interrupted by a knock at the door.

It was a delicate knock – one that immediately said child rather than adult – and, had anyone been talking, we might not have even heard it.

Don, being closest to the door, went to see who it was, and seeing him looking down – I couldn't actually see who was there – I knew my hunch had been correct. I also recognised the voice. It was Shona.

Don ushered her in. 'Miss Vickers sent me,' she said nervously, eyeing the strangers in the room. 'She wondered if it would be possible for Mrs Watson to come down to the Unit …' She glanced at me and then back to Don. 'Only it's Ben, and he's …'

'What's happened, Shona?' I began. But Jim was already rising. 'No, no, leave this one to me, Mrs Watson,' he said, shrugging his jacket from the back of his chair. 'You carry on. You're the one who's going to be working with Imogen, so it makes much more sense for me to go and deal with it – whatever "it" is. What's he been up to, Shona?'

I could see Shona looking doubtful. She glanced at me again. 'It's him and Henry,' she said. 'They've been fighting, and now Ben's locked in the art cupboard. The one by the water fountain … but Miss Vickers said …'

'Locked *in*?' Gary asked her. 'By who?'

Shona shook her head. 'I don't know,' she said. 'Miss Vickers didn't tell me. Just that she needed Mrs Watson to come.' She glanced at me again.

Jim had come around the table now, and I found myself in something of a quandary. I knew Jim could handle it – I knew Jim could handle anything (better than I could, in many cases) – but I got the distinct impression that it was specifically *me* Kelly wanted to come and sort it. And knowing Ben so much better now, I also thought I knew why. But to point that out, in this company, would have been highly inappropriate, so I held my tongue.

But Gary must have seen something in either my or Shona's expressions that made him realise it was me who needed to go.

'No, no, thanks, but I think it'll be best if you stay here, Mr Dawson,' he said decisively. 'We've still got Josh Harrison to talk about, haven't we?' He nodded towards me. 'Go on, Mrs Watson – we're all but done here, anyway, I think. We've got another meeting scheduled next week to discuss the action plan for Imogen, haven't we, Mr Swift?' He looked at the senior social worker, who nodded.

'Yes,' he confirmed. 'We're just waiting on the speech therapist's report, basically.'

I needed no further invitation. I stood up, grabbed my bag, said my farewells and left with Shona.

So,' I said, hotfooting it down the corridor alongside her, 'as they say on American cop shows, what's been going down?'

Quite a lot, it seemed. Shona, as it turned out, could tell me very little. Only that Ben and Henry had started fighting and it had all got very 'shouty', and Miss Vickers had stopped it and made the boys apologise to each other, but then Henry had done something and Ben had attacked him with a pair of scissors and he was now locked in the art cupboard by the water fountain.

I.e. the one just down the corridor from my classroom. Where there was a drawer with a key in it that opened the art cupboard. The question was, who'd done the locking and who had the key now?

'Oh, Ben himself,' Kelly told me, once we'd settled the children with their workbooks and had popped just outside the door to discuss it out of earshot. 'No one's locked him in there. He's locked himself in. Little tyke must have slipped round and grabbed it while my back was turned. He was out of the classroom like a flipping whippet and it was only because I wasn't far from the door that I followed him out in time to seem him go in there. Had I not, he could have been there indefinitely, because it was the last place I would have thought of looking – I'd have assumed he'd have scarpered altogether.' She glanced down the corridor.

'Mind you, he still might be in there for an indefinite period because, Ben being Ben, he's intent on staying there, as well.' She smiled, albeit grimly. 'Currently he's running it like a kind of hostage situation. Refusing to negotiate terms for the release of sugar paper and poster paint till his demands are met.'

'Which are?'

'Straightforward. That he won't get' – she raised fingers into quote marks – ''scluded.'

Her expression became more serious, then. 'He went for Henry, Casey. Didn't hurt him badly, as far as I can see – no flesh wounds or anything. But he has definitely gone at him with a pair of scissors – Molly witnessed it – and, of course, he's had his nine lives, hasn't he? And he knows it. That's what I'm guessing this is about.'

I realised I'd been right in my hunch that this was something I should deal with. This was something I had a better chance of diffusing – or at least minimising, or not making worse, anyway – than Jim did, because the one thing that I'd learned in the weeks Ben had been with us was that Ben didn't react to discipline from male teachers nearly as well as female ones. In fact, from his notes – which I'd read – there was a definite pattern. He would invariably lash out, and make things worse for himself. It was almost instinctive, I reckoned, and in all probability related to his home life; one in which the primary male in it – the *only* male – spent much of his time shouting at his only child and, from what the paperwork said, more often than not while inebriated.

Not that Jim would shout – far from it; he was one of those effortlessly authoritative teachers who barely needed to raise their voices, ever – but with Ben and I having such a rapport building between us now, I knew I was best placed both to coax him from the cupboard and glean enough information to make an informed judgement about how serious an incident this had actually been. Though it couldn't be that bad, surely? Yes, we had scissors in the classroom, but they were blunt-ended *and* blunt. They could barely manage medium-grade card. Still, it was a dispiriting bit of news, this, and potentially another blot on his copy-book, and I hoped his crucial ninth life hadn't *quite* expired yet.

'And I'm sorry to call you away from your meeting,' Kelly added. 'Only the caretaker's nowhere to be found – I sent Shona up there first – and I thought it better to drag you out of your meeting than start calling out the cavalry. Given the situation with him and everything ...'

'You did good.' I grinned, touching a finger to my temple. 'You used your nous. You will go far, my child. Right, then. If you can hold the fort, onwards to the cupboard!'

What was it with me and keys lately? I thought, as I stationed myself outside the art cupboard door and gently knocked. First Imogen, locking me in, and now Ben, locking me out. Was there some sort of message I should be taking from all this?

'Ben, love,' I called softly, grateful that we weren't quite at the end of the second period yet and that the corridor was therefore empty of marauding teenagers. 'Ben, it's me.'

I put my ear to the door. Nothing. Was he even still in there? Was there a chance he could have scarpered while the coast was clear? No, I realised. Imogen – oblivious, ironically, that she was the subject of our meeting – had been stationed by my classroom door when we'd got back there, no doubt with the express instruction from Kelly to keep it in view. 'Ben,' I said again, more forcefully, 'it's me and I need to speak to you. Come on, at least let me know you're there. One knock for yes, two for no ...' I paused. 'And three for ...'

There were two knocks. So he hadn't lost his sense of humour.

'Okay, then,' I said. 'So we have two choices. Either you come out, or I come in. I don't mind which, but you need to choose one or I am going to have to go and find the caretaker and that's going to put him in a very bad mood.'

'I didn't do it!' came the unequivocal response.

'Didn't do what?' I asked.

'Didn't do what Henry said I did. He's a liar!'

'What did Henry say you did?'

'He said I stabbed him, an' I didn't!'

'I haven't spoken to Henry yet, Ben,' I said. 'I wanted to speak to you first. I want you tell me what happened. From the beginning.'

There was a pause, and I could hear a bit of banging and scraping. 'You on your own?' he demanded finally. 'You haven't brought no one, have you?' It seemed I wasn't the only one who watched cop shows.

'Entirely alone,' I said. 'Though the bell's due to go in ... let me see ... 12 minutes. At which point I won't be on

my own any more. There will be several dozen pupils passing by, thinking I'm talking to a door. So. Shall I come in
there, so you can tell me?'

More bangings and scrapings. He'd obviously used his
time productively, by barricading himself in. Then, to my
delight, I heard the key scrape in the lock.

'Shove along, then,' I said, as the door opened to reveal
one rather dishevelled and tremulous 11-year-old boy, with
a face streaked with tear tracks and chalk dust.

It was a bit of a squeeze, there having been a recent deliv-
ery, but I managed to perch my backside on the bottom-
most shelf, cushioned by a pile of coloured A3 sheets of
card. Opposite me, the shelves were crammed in preparation for the usual New Year display drive with rolls of foil
paper, border ribbon and big plastic bottles of poster paint,
as well as the more workaday packs of sugar paper, model-
ling clay and white cartridge. It smelt good, a smell I always
associated with enthusiasm and creative endeavour. Though
with a definite top-note of sweaty pre-pubescent boy.

'So what happened, Ben?' I asked him. 'Truthfully, okay?
No making up things. Everyone was in the classroom, so
people saw it, okay?' I held his gaze, to be sure he took in
what I was saying. 'So, go on. Let's have it. From the
beginning.'

And it seemed Ben was happy enough to tell me. Henry
had started it (predictably – it was rare for these kids to ever
confess to 'starting' anything) by taking a particular felt
pen, which Ben had been using and had only put down for
a minute, and when he'd tried to take it back Henry had
grabbed it, and somehow it had ended up making a mark

on the desk, and of course, it being a permanent marker and there being rules about permanent markers, both boys had accused the other of marking the desk and it had got out of hand, culminating in a full-on fist fight, which Kelly had called a halt to.

As often happened, however, even though both boys had apologised, there'd still been some residual needle about who'd been most at fault, and somehow – Ben was characteristically reticent about precise details – it had flared up again. And as Ben had had scissors in his hands at the time, he'd jabbed them towards Henry – but only in retaliation (honest, Miss!) after Henry had poked him in the ribs with a recently sharpened pencil.

'An' no one saw *that*!' Ben protested, beginning to cry now. 'No one saw that, Miss – an' it was sharp and it hurt! And I didn't hurt him – I only threatened him an … they were plastic scissors, anyway! An … an …' he could barely speak for crying now, 'an' if he tells and says I did,' he gulped, 'and I get 'scluded from this school as well, I'm gonna be put in a children's home!'

The last word came out as a sob – the tears were streaming down his face now – and it occurred to me that nowhere, in this tiny temple to paper of all kinds, would there be anything as useful as a tissue. Tissue paper, yes, but nothing he could blow his nose with.

But he'd already addressed that by the time I had checked all my pockets, by tugging down one of his frayed sweatshirt cuffs and raking it across his wet face.

'Sweetheart,' I said, 'whatever makes you say such a thing? Who said you're going to get excluded?'

'Henry did!'

'Well, last time I looked the name on the headmaster's office wasn't Henry Davis. And what's all this about being put in a children's home?'

This prompted a fresh bout of sobbing. 'That's what he *said*!'

'What, Henry did?'

'No, my *dad* did! He's already been on to the child-catcher lady. He said if I get into any more trouble at school he's ringing her and getting shot of me. He did!'

'Ben, I'm sure he didn't mean that –'

'Yes he did,' he gulped. 'He's made the 'pointment and everything.'

'What appointment?'

'He said he phoned the lady and they said that if he has any more nonsense he can ring the Childline and get me picked up in a van.'

'Ben, listen to me. Childline's for *children*. For children to call if they have problems and they need someone to talk to.'

'That's what I thought,' he sniffed, 'but it isn't, Miss. If you ring Childline they can come and take you away. And I know it because I've seen it, Miss. I have. There was a boy in our flats – he rang Childline and no one never saw him again. Never.'

I took a deep breath then, feeling a familiar sense of frustration and impotent anger rise within me. Anger at the adults who could possibly think it a sensible idea to put such terrible nonsense in gullible children's heads.

'Ben,' I said, standing up and placing a hand on each of

his shoulders, 'listen to me, now, okay? Firstly, Childline don't take children away. They *help* children – help children who are in difficult situations, and sometimes, yes, that means that they *do* leave their homes – but only if they need to go to a better, safer place. And secondly,' I added, hoping my instinct was correct, 'I don't think for a *second* that your dad wants to put you in a children's home. Yes, he's scared you,' I said, 'making you think that …' I paused, knowing I shouldn't go too far. It wasn't for me to pass judgement on his disciplining style, after all – not to Ben, at any rate. 'But that's *not* going to happen, okay? And thirdly,' – I knew I was on much surer ground now – 'you are *not* going to be excluded for what happened with Henry, okay?'

Ben sniffed. 'Honest, Miss?'

'Honest, Ben,' I said firmly. 'Yes, you did wrong – you both did. Because we don't resolve our differences by fighting with each other, do we? Neither do we threaten each other with pencils and scissors. And you will both come into school early for the rest of the week, to help clear leaves and litter-pick with the caretaker. And you will both apologise, too – firstly to Miss Vickers, for disrupting her lesson, *and* to each other.'

He nodded again. And I was pleased to see that the sweatshirt cuff was now substantially wetter than his face was – because he had, at last, stopped crying.

'So,' I said, 'what we're going to do is this. We're going to go to the toilets, so you can wash your face, okay? Then we're going to go back to the Unit, and while everyone else has their break you and I and Henry are going to sort this out.'

And then I (a thought I didn't share, while Ben wiped his face again) was going to go and make a mental note – and perhaps also an actual one – about speaking to Gary about us speaking to Ben's father, to see if we couldn't at least have a quiet word about what seemed, under the circumstances, to be a rather counter-productive approach to disciplining his only, not to mention motherless, child.

Humph, I thought, as the bell went. 'Child-catcher lady' indeed. No wonder social workers got such a bad press.

# Chapter 19

With everything calming down on the child-protection front now, we were in something of a lull; it had definitely become that in-betweeny time of year. The excitement of Bonfire Night (and the stress of it) now seemed like a distant memory and had been replaced with a period of time that seemed dark and interminable, but at the same time not quite long enough to get everything done for the run-up to Christmas.

I was thrilled that everything seemed to be getting sorted for the most troubled of my troubled students, and now she was talking reasonably freely I was keen to get to know her better, but I never seemed to have a minute these days. It seemed there was an endless round of meetings, and the whiff of change was in the air; something that was a natural part of school life, and Unit life in particular, but it never made it seem less than unsettling.

We'd had a meeting to discuss progress generally, once the whole Imogen situation had been addressed, and preparations had been made for Gavin, Henry and Shona to return to mainstream classes in the New Year. All were ready, but all were still nervous about the prospect, and I felt for them. I worried about Gavin in particular, as he had more than once threatened (well, at least confided in me that he had threatened) to stop taking his medication to make himself 'bad' again, so that he could stay with me.

On top of all this, it seemed, I was getting a new child in my unit. A 14-year-old girl.

'Though it's just a case of containment really,' Julia Styles, the school SENCO, had assured me when she popped down to let me know there was a new pupil imminent. 'There aren't any problems that we know of other than that the girl – her name is Gemma, by the way – is partially sighted. She doesn't use a cane, but she does need a hand getting around the place until she feels confident enough to do it herself.'

'And there's really no one else to help?' I asked.

It wasn't that I was opposed to the idea, but I just didn't see how much help I could be, particularly due to the fact that it transpired that she was also above average intelligence. 'If she's with us in the Unit, she'll miss out on a chunk of her education, won't she? I mean, she's welcome, of course, but it will be almost impossible to set special lessons just for her, not at this late stage in the term.'

'I know – it's not ideal, is it?' Julia agreed. 'But, unfortunately, we don't really have a choice. And if she misses out on anything vital, I'm sure we can catch her up in the New Year, can't we? It's just that we've secured funding for a special TA to come in full time for her, and she's on top of the specialist equipment required – some kind of speaking computer system – but unfortunately, she can't start until mid-January.'

So that was that. I was going to lose three and gain one, which would make the place feel very quiet. Only I wasn't losing the three just yet, and Gemma was set to join us the following day. Which I thought was a pretty silly time of year to be starting in a new school, until I read the notes Julia left me and I realised that Gemma and her family had just moved to the area – literally that week – to start a new life for themselves, after fighting for years to keep their daughter in a mainstream school.

So, for a bit, at least, it was going to be even busier. So I spent the rest of the morning looking at the schedule to see if I could carve out some special time for her, while the children were happily (always a bonus with my volatile little crew) making cards and decorations.

I was so engrossed that it was almost lunchtime before I knew it, and was only made aware of the time by Shona appearing at my desk. I also noticed a sudden hush had fallen and that she was obviously the spokesperson for them all. 'Here, Miss,' she said, placing a card on my desk, which smelt of pine and was still gluey in places. 'Me and the others have made this for you to take home,' she said, colouring slightly. 'It's just to say thanks for looking after us, and because I'm gonna miss you next term.'

'I will too, Miss!' Gavin called across, waving from the boys' table.

In fact, it wasn't only Gavin. All the children were watching me. Then Henry also called out, 'I'll miss you too, Miss!'

I looked at what Shona had laid on the desk and I had to gulp hard to swallow the lump forming in my throat. While I had thought they were making paper chains and decorations to hang in the classroom, they had obviously spent much of their time creating what was in front of me now. It was a big gold heart, made from card, and all around the edges, neatly glued, were carefully drawn, painted and cut-out sprigs of holly and berries. Then, inside the heart, like the openings on an advent calendar, were little windows, behind which was an individual message from each of the children. It was a lost cause, trying not to cry in such a situation, so I didn't. 'Look at me,' I sniffed. 'I can hardly see to read your messages!' Though I could see enough to make out *I'll miss you lots, like jelly tots*, from Shona, and *Your my favrit teacher*, from little Ben, but the one that struck me as most poignant was from Imogen, which really got me going, because it simply said *Thank you for helping me find my voice*.

'Oh, you guys! Look at me!' I said, reaching for my bag so I could stanch the flow with tissues. 'You've got me in a right mess! Oh this is *so* lovely. Thank you all so much. And, you know what? What with everything being so busy, I haven't even thought about putting up my tree yet, but now you've made me feel all Christmassy, so I'm going to get everything out as soon as I get home tonight, and this,' I added, picking up my card, 'is going to have pride of place, right in the middle of my mantelpiece.'

I then got up from my desk and went round and gave each of them a hug, before stashing my card safely between two stout pieces of card, to go in my satchel, and, once the bell went, fairly skipping to the staffroom. Where, equally pleasingly, there were warm mince pies up for grabs.

Kelly was already wellying into her second. 'You know what you should do?' she said, when I told her about the new girl who'd be joining the following morning. 'You should delegate, that's what you should do.'

I took a mince pie as well. 'I was planning on doing that anyway, once I'd wrestled your timetable off you.'

'No, not to me,' she said. 'Though, obviously, that's taken as read anyway. No, I was thinking you should delegate responsibility for helping this new girl to one of the *other* kids.'

'One of the others?'

'*Yes*. You know, you really ought to take a leaf out of your Kieron's book,' Kelly responded, with a cheeky wink. 'You know how you say he always sees the simplest solution?' I nodded. 'Well, it *is* simple. This new TA is starting in the middle of January, right? And you have Shona returning to classes at the beginning of January, and in the meantime you designate Shona as official looker-after, you know; taking her where she needs to be, being her eyes as and where necessary, and even better – "Now that's why this is a *great* idea, Kelly." "Thanks, Casey! Don't mention it" – you should put Shona in charge and make Imogen her assistant, promoting Imogen to main looker-after once we come back after Christmas, and thereby killing two birds with one stone. Ta da! What do you think? Brilliant, eh?'

'You little genius!' I said, clapping Kelly on the back, causing her to spit out a little dust-storm of pastry crumbs. 'You're absolutely right. That *is* bloody brilliant, and it completely solves the problem of Imogen feeling bereft once Shona's gone.'

'Um, hello? Of course I'm right. I invariably am. Though thanks for that,' she said, coughing delicately and brushing crumbs from her trousers. 'I was enjoying that mince pie.'

'I was just thinking of your hips, love,' I said with a wink. 'Let me see – was that your second or your third?'

As days went, that particular one couldn't have got a lot better, though there was less festive cheer when the family all got home to find themselves press-ganged into all-hands-on-deck-decorating-assistant mode, and expected to take orders from me.

'Mother! I do have a life you know,' Riley complained as she checked her watch for the umpteenth time. I had put her in charge of assembling one of the four artificial trees we'd amassed over the years – not to mention the real one I'd already sent Mike to buy and which he was now busy stabilising in its bucket. 'I promised David faithfully that I wouldn't be late for his parents' drinks and canapés evening – and don't give me that look. You already *knew* this!'

'It's not a look. It's an "Ooh, get you and your canapés!" All sounds very posh.' I threw her a box. 'Just one more set of lights around this window and you are officially dismissed. Gawd, though. They're coming on Boxing Day, aren't they? I hope we're not going to have to put on airs and graces or, indeed, canapés, when they visit …'

'Yes, mother, I know: "They'll have to take us as they find us." You've told me that five times already!'

She knew I was only teasing because she was so easy to wind up, but perhaps I'd gone overboard with the all hands on deck thing, because it was getting late, and now she'd missed her bus.

'Don't worry, love!' Mike chirruped. 'I'll take you, no problem!' simultaneously flinging down the string of lights he'd been trying to untangle, the relief in his face telling me he'd rather do anything than help turn the house into Santa's grotto.

'Oh well, that's just great!' I scolded, and then turned to Kieron, who was busy keeping his head down and attaching baubles to one of the trees. 'And I suppose you have something super-urgent you need to be doing too?' I asked him.

Kieron picked up a Santa hat and placed it on his head. 'Have no fear, Mum,' he said, 'because your Christmas elf is here. And you know what?' he added, *sotto voce*. 'We'll get it done a *lot* quicker and with a great deal less stress. Riley just moans on' – he duly ducked – 'and Dad is – sorry, Dad – basically rubbish.'

He was right, too. And, surprise, surprise, they didn't need telling twice. They were out of there before you could say ho, ho, ho.

# Chapter 20

The new girl turned out to be a sweetheart. And something of a role model as well. She definitely found something of a one-boy fan-club in Gavin, who was so intrigued by all the whats and whys and wherefores of her sight problems that he followed her round like an enthusiastic puppy, wanting a running commentary on what she could see and couldn't see, and to know whether she'd developed some sort of laser-sonar thing.

She also took to Shona straight away – well, who wouldn't? – and once we put her in the picture she was gentle and patient with Imogen, who was so impressed by the way she seemed to deal with her disability that I thought – though didn't say, because it wasn't even necessary – that it was even making her reflect on the communication challenges *she'd* faced, and giving her a much-needed injection of positivity about it all.

'She's coming on in leaps and bounds, in fact,' I told Mr Swift at our next meeting just a week before we broke up.

'She's speaking in all the sorts of situations you'd expect her to when she's in the Unit – and she's taken really well to having a clearly defined role, where she has to use her voice, too.' I explained about the new girl, Gemma, and how she was helping out with her, and how much this had given her confidence a boost.

'That's extremely good to hear,' Mr Swift said. 'And we're confident she'll be able to move back with her father in the New Year – well, on a part-time basis, anyway. With him being on his own, and with the kind of work he does, it's not going to be feasible for her to live with him full time at the moment. But his parents are happy to continue to look after her when their son is out of the country, or working away elsewhere, so, all being well, we'll be able to be out of their hair early in the New Year.'

I smiled at this. I had yet to even meet Imogen's father – which was ironic, given everything – but social services were clearly all over him like a rash. That was the thing with social services – once they were involved, they had no choice but to be in a family's hair. And until such time as they were happy that the child or children in question were having their needs met, of course. That was what they were there for; not as child-catchers, but as child-advocates. Yes, it was great to know Imogen was going to be able to live with her dad again, as she'd clearly never wanted to be parted from him, but for all his apparent guilt and remorse about it afterwards, the truth still remained that he'd left her in the care of a woman who not only didn't care for her, but actively mistreated her. And would no doubt have continued to do so, by the sound of it – she was having a bit of a free ride, after all – had Imogen herself not responded with perhaps the most unlikely cry for help: a selective shut-down in actually crying for help at *all*.

So it was all positive, but as I left the meeting to return to the Unit it didn't escape my notice that there was still a big hole in Imogen's life, and one which she had so far refused to open up about at all: her real mother. Where exactly did she fit into all this? And had Imogen ever really been spoken to about her disappearance? I decided that it wouldn't hurt to give Mrs Hinchcliffe another ring, both to update her on how things had been going in school – yes, Imogen was doing well, but it was important to keep up the momentum – and to see if she would open up about the other Mrs Hinchcliffe, at all.

And, to my delight, she sounded positively enthused.

'Yes, of course, dear,' she said, when I phoned her during the lunch break to see if I could perhaps pop round with a progress report.

'He's not been the best of choosers, has he?' Mrs Hinchcliffe told me, pouring tea from her striped teapot two afternoons later. The kitchen felt so much warmer now – for me, perhaps a little too warm – but it wasn't just about the temperature; the whole house seemed to have a different feel to it. Not being as manic as I was, the Hinchcliffes had yet to put up any Christmas decorations, but the place definitely had a more relaxed and happy air about it. I also noticed that the fridge had been adorned with evidence of Imogen's various activities; there was a calendar on it, in which dates had been circled and things scribbled, as well as an invitation to a birthday party which I could see was addressed to her. There was also a photo – of Imogen and her dad, somewhere in the countryside, both wearing beany hats and pulling goofy faces, and a self-portrait, carefully drawn, and showing quite a degree of artistic talent, that I recognised as being part of a project we'd done in school.

Fridges, I thought – you could probably do some really useful science using fridges. Well, if not science, exactly, at least do some amateur psychology – because I'd seen lots of fridges in my time, and had owned a few, too – and they seemed to me to be a fairly reliable indicator of a family's emotional health. And with this family, you could see that Imogen *lived* here, now – lived here properly. Was no longer a challenging temporary visitor for a pair of well-intentioned but frazzled grandparents. No, she was a part of the fabric of the house now. You could feel her presence here. Feel an acceptance, a kind of calm and bedding-in.

I smiled to myself while Mrs Hinchcliffe opened the fridge and plucked a bottle of milk from inside the door. Well, calm for the moment, at least. The next stage, assuming she continued to split her time between her dad's home and her grandparents', would be the maelstrom that might ensue once those teenage hormones started kicking in. That said, they'd already had a dose of door slamming and ranting, hadn't they? So at least they wouldn't be going into it completely cold.

I accepted my cup of tea and stirred it while Mrs Hinchcliffe sat down in the other chair. 'No,' she said again, 'poor Graham's not got much savvy when it comes to women. Though, fair play, we were taken in by that terrible woman, too, but I'm afraid our Graham never did have much skill when it came to girlfriends.'

'Third time lucky?' I quipped.

'Third time over my flipping dead body!' she said with surprising forcefulness. Then she smiled. 'Oh, it's his life,' she said, 'and that's fine, and of course we want to see him happy, but all the while he's got Fanny Adams to think about, I'll be taking a dim view if he thinks he's bringing anyone else home. And so will his father,' she added. '*And* he knows it.' She chuckled.

'I'm sure he'll think twice,' I said. 'He's been through a hard time as well, hasn't he? It must have been a heck of a shock for him when it all came to light.'

She nodded. 'I know I'm his mother, and I'm biased, but he deserves so much better. But he's too soft. That's his problem. That's why Mick's always despaired of him. Lets women walk all over him. Far too much the romantic.'

'Was that what his first wife did?' I ventured.

'Her?' she almost spat the word out. 'Walked on him with knobs on, did that one, then trampled on him again for good measure.'

'What happened?'

'Same thing that always happens,' said Mrs Hinchcliffe with a sniff. 'Had an affair, didn't she? Cat's away and all that – and he was away all the time, of course. Trying to earn a bob or two to support them all. And that's how she repaid him. Just upped and went to France, with some divorced man from her office. Just disappeared. No note. No explanation. No nothing.'

'To France?'

'Yes, he was half-French, this fancy man she took up with. First we knew of it – and remember, little Imogen was only just 11 then – was when she phoned him a couple of weeks later to say she wasn't coming back.'

'But what about Imogen?'

'Exactly! Can you imagine any mother ever doing that?'

I shook my head even though, from what I'd seen over the past couple of years – not to mention the past couple of months – sadly I could.

'Exactly,' she said again. 'But she did. Decided she was too young – which she was; still had a lot of growing up to do, that one – and of course she blamed him for getting her pregnant, like they always do.' She sniffed again. 'Then decided that since she couldn't afford to visit, it would be better to have a so-called "clean" break. *Clean break*? I ask you, since when did any little one want a clean break from their own mother? Heartbreaking, it was. Criminal. And if you want my opinion there was a bit more to it that that. I reckon – and Mick agrees – that it was more a case of that man of hers laying the law down. You come on your own or you don't come at all, sort of thing. Still, she made her choice and that's for her to have to live with, isn't it? Our Imogen's managing okay without her.'

And, on balance, for the moment at least, she was probably right about that. Perhaps she'd come and find her daughter one day and perhaps they'd build some bridges, but, right now, Imogen had close relatives who loved her dearly and wanted only the best for her – something several of the kids who passed through my Unit had never had, and sadly might never have.

'She's more than managing,' I told Mrs Hinchcliffe. 'In fact, in the last few weeks she's been blossoming. It's been wonderful to see how confident she's becoming. How's she been at home? Has she talked very much about Gerri?'

Mrs Hinchcliffe shook her head. 'Not at all,' she said, 'but least said soonest mended, in my book. Though she still has her psychologist woman coming round once a week. So she might speak to her, of course. But to us, no. I think she just wants to forget it. And as Mick says ...' She paused then, looking past me, towards the hallway. 'Speak of the devil. There he is.'

I turned around to see Mr Hinchcliffe pushing the door open, with Imogen just behind him, then slipping a couple of carrier bags off his wrists and down onto the doormat. In his other hand he held what looked at first glance like a collection of firewood. Except it wasn't. It was an armful of planks.

'Don't you think you're traipsing in here with all that!' said Mrs Hinchcliffe. 'Go on – take it round the side. I've only hoovered an hour since, for goodness' sake. I'm not having you dropping sawdust all over the carpet.'

She turned to me then. 'Men and their blinking hobbies,' she said. 'You should see the state of our garage. Pain in the flipping proverbial.'

I laughed and stood up. It was probably time to leave. Imogen was still taking off her coat and boots in the hall as I went to slip mine on again. She smiled. 'Oh, hi, Miss. What you doing here?'

'Just popped in to see your nan for a catch-up,' I said. 'That's all. You all organised for Christmas?'

Imogen grinned, her cheeks two little pink apples from the cold. 'I think we are. I've been helping my nan – we've made mince pies and sausage rolls *and* a Christmas cake. If you call round again before Christmas, you could try one if you like.'

Bless her, I thought. 'I'll bet they'll be delicious, too,' I said. 'There's always something special about cakes baked by nans and their granddaughters. It's the extra love, I think. That's what my nan used to say. So I'll bear it in mind if I'm passing and feeling peckish. In the meantime, I had better get going. I've got mince pies of my own to bake as soon as I get back. Now, if I could only rustle up a granddaughter, I'd be laughing ...'

# Chapter 21

'I hope you're leaving some of those for me,' Kieron called out from the hall, as I transferred mince pies from tin to Tupperware container the following morning, ready to take into school with me.

'I might,' I called back. 'If you're very, very good.'

'Mum, I am *always* good,' he said, appearing in front of me with his arms full of mysterious leads and cables. Who knew what he got up to at college? It was mostly Greek to me, but whatever it was it definitely seemed to suit him. 'Name me one incidence,' he went on, 'in the last, erm, let me see ... six months – yes, six *months* – when I have done anything whatsoever that has annoyed you in any way.'

I smiled to myself. That was Kieron all over. He had the sort of memory that catalogued everything down to the tiniest detail. You could never say something like 'Remember that time when ...' unless you were 100 per cent accurate about details. Especially when it came to anything that might make him anxious, like getting a telling-off from Mike for some minor misdemeanour or other – he'd be able to quote him verbatim.

'What's with this whole domestic goddess bit anyway, Mum?' Riley wanted to know. 'Did someone come in to school with a cake and make you feel all inadequate?'

'Cheeky mare!' I said. 'This is nothing to do with feeling inadequate – or me trying to be a domestic goddess either. They're for our party, if you must know. We've got the carol service today and after they've done their performance we're going to have a little end-of-term Christmas party during last period.'

'Aww, I remember those days so well,' Kieron said, looking wistful.

'I'd hope so,' Riley said. 'You've only left the place five blooming minutes!'

'But it seems so long *ago*,' he continued. 'Carol services and mince pies and not having to worry about anything but remembering to get your homework book signed …'

'Which you mostly didn't,' I chipped in.

'Welcome to my world, little bro,' Riley said. 'It's called the *real* one.' She reached past me and pinched a mince pie from the tin. 'Mum,' she said, '*how* many kids did you say you have in that Unit of yours? You look like you're planning on feeding the five thousand!'

'Seven, currently,' I told her, 'but I won't just be feeding them, will I? I'll be lucky to get away with less than about 30. And you know what it's like; they'll be gone before you can say *Oh, Little Town of Bethlehem*, trust me.'

And it was a problem of my own making, to be fair, because I'd been a bit free and easy with sending out invitations. But that was the way a support structure such as the Unit *should* work, to my mind. Children came and went, but, whatever happened next, the one thing they all went away *with* was the security of knowing that the Unit door was always open.

I'd also made a point of getting in touch with the parents and guardians of my current brood, both to encourage them to come along and see their children perform at the church and to join us for our little 'after-show' as well. It wasn't the usual way of things, but Mr Moore was becoming used to me by now, and fully agreed with my idea that it was a good way to foster good relations with parents who were often struggling with their children themselves.

'Anyway, you don't need to worry,' I told them both, while Kieron managed to snake out a hand from under his cable spaghetti and grab a couple too. 'I seem to have made half a zillion of the things, thanks to your auntie Donna's enormous stock of mincemeat, so you won't be missing out. You'll be sick of the things by Christmas eve.'

'Mum,' said Kieron, 'remember what Aristotle said.'

'Aristotle? What on earth did he have to say on the subject of mince pies?'

'Nothing. But he did say that nature abhors a vacuum. Which means if there's a gap you should fill it. Ergo, there is *always* room for a mince pie.'

It had been a tense couple of weeks, and I didn't doubt there would have been some tears before bedtime, but we had finally reached a point where I was reasonably confident that our little Unit would acquit ourselves well. Because what we were doing today – singing *Oh, Little Town of Bethlehem*, on our own, at the carol service – was a completely new departure. But not a completely random one; it had been inspired in part by my research into selective mutism, in fact, and a snippet I'd read about speech problems generally, and how things like singing were often easier to cope with than talking.

It had made for fascinating reading, too – learning just how singing could be used as therapy – and also how children with problems such as stammers often found it much easier to sing than speak, and profoundly autistic kids, who could barely speak at all, could sometimes memorise and sing whole songs, like angels. Essentially, though, I just liked the idea of my brood learning a carol, rehearsing it diligently and then actually performing it in public. It just struck me as another confidence string they would have to their bows. Well, if they pulled it off, that was.

So it was also a little scary, as was any venture into the unknown, and given that my little brood found even mainstream classes difficult (for their various reasons) I hoped I hadn't been too ambitious in expecting them to memorise a whole carol, let alone perform it in front of a church congregation. And without – in some cases, anyway – resorting to any silliness or bad behaviour.

But I remained confident. I'd taken my cue from the special needs department, who every year put on an impressive assembly, in which awards were given out for various special needs pupils, and the rest of the school were also entertained.

This would be on a much smaller scale, obviously, but it would also be a good way to test the water, and, who knew? If it went well, maybe we could expand on it. After all, the children we looked after shared one big disadvantage – the very fact of them being sent to me already made them feel they'd failed in some way. It didn't matter why they'd come to me – whether they were the bullies, the chronically shy, the challenging or the challenged – they all shared that sense of being out of the mainstream which, in itself, made a dent in their self-esteem.

And this was one way to give them some back.

'If they don't clam up completely in fright,' Kelly observed as our little crocodile finished the ten-minute walk from school to church a couple of hours later. No, it wasn't Westminster Cathedral exactly, but it wasn't a tiny chapel either and, more importantly, it was already filling up. This was one of the few days in the year when they could be sure of being packed to the rafters. Judging by the number of people we could see filing in – young mums, various relatives, a large percentage of the local elderly population – there didn't look like being an empty pew anywhere.

'They'll be fine,' I said, as we ushered the children round to the church hall behind, where the main school choir had already assembled. 'You'll be fine, kids,' I repeated. 'Remember what I said. What are you going to do?'

'We're going to steal the show, Miss!' came Gavin's excited response, drowning out pretty much everyone else.

'Well, as long as he doesn't take that *too* literally,' Kelly whispered. 'Did you bring his lunchtime pill by the way?'

I grinned, and was just patting my handbag reassuringly when Shona came over. She'd been spending more time with her old class over the past few days, in readiness for her return, and was also in the school choir already, but I'd seconded her as my own unofficial choirmaster as I knew her presence would help Imogen with her nerves.

Though there wasn't much to be done about mine …

'Caught you crying,' Kelly ribbed me, waving her camera in my face as we made our way back out to the church hall. I was buzzing – not to mention still slightly in shock that it had all gone so incredibly well.

'Oi!' I said. 'You were supposed to be filming the performance, not panning round the audience getting pap shots of unsuspecting wailing women!'

'Couldn't resist,' she said. 'And I can always edit you out – at a price, obviously. Seriously, though – how about our Imogen, then?'

I nodded and began rootling in my handbag for a tissue.

'That was what set me off. I just couldn't help thinking what a lovely picture it made. You know? Imogen belting out *Oh, Morning Stars, to-ge-e-e-ether* – gawd, did she go for it, or what? And in front of an audience, too, don't forget. Amazing. Specially when you think that only three months ago she couldn't say a single word. Ah,' I said, 'speak of the devil. There's the Hinchcliffes. I'll just nip over and remind them about the party. Back in two ticks.'

The church hall had filled up fast now the service was over and by the time I'd crossed it, threading my way through the scores of chattering pupils and parents, saying hellos and well dones here and there, Mrs Hinchcliffe was deep in conversation with Henry's mum, and Mr Hinchcliffe seemed to be chatting with Imogen and – somewhat unexpectedly – with Henry.

Mr Hinchcliffe, who was facing me, nodded a hello. I tapped Henry, who had his back to me, on the shoulder. 'Chop, chop,' I said. 'Shouldn't you two be heading back to line up with Miss Vickers?' I asked him and Imogen. 'We've got a party to get organised, after all.'

'We are, Miss,' he said. 'We're going now, aren't we, Im? We're just sorting out tea first, Miss.'

'Tea?' I looked from one to the other.

Mr Hinchcliffe nodded. 'Henry's coming round this weekend, aren't you, lad?'

Henry nodded happily.

'Is that right?' I said, intrigued by this development. 'That's nice.'

'And we've been making a sledge, Miss, haven't we, Imogen? With Imogen's grandad.'

'Are you now?' I said.

Imogen shook her head. 'No, *he's* helping grandad make the sledge, Miss. I just do the watching.'

'And you're on tea duty, remember,' her grandfather was quick to point out. 'Anyway, chop, chop, like Mrs Watson says,' he said, running a hand over the top of Imogen's head. 'We'll see you in school in a bit, love, okay?'

'So Saturday's all right, is it?' Henry wanted to know.

'Yes, Henry. Saturday's fine. Any time after lunch.'

I watched them skip across the church hall to join the others, then turned back to Mr Hinchcliffe. 'Didn't she do well?'

'That she did,' he said. 'More than well, actually. Had her nan filling up, she did. She's a good girl …'

'She's certainly that, Mr Hinchcliffe,' I agreed. 'We're all so proud of her. She's come on so well, hasn't she? Even better than we expected, especially when you think what she's been through … still, we can put that all behind us now, can't we? And you're making a sledge for her, are you? Lucky girl.'

Mr Hinchcliffe smiled and nodded over towards the children. 'Me and my little helper,' he said, nodding. 'He's a nice lad, that Henry. Good with his hands, too. Keen to learn.'

I agreed that he was – well, at least some of the time anyway. He tended not to be quite so keen when it came to doing sums rather than sledges. And as I did so I could see that Mr Hinchcliffe had something of a twinkle in his eye. It seemed it wasn't only Imogen, perhaps, who'd found herself a friend. 'We just need some snow now so they can use the flipping thing,' he finished. Then he chuckled, tipping his head back before shaking it bemusedly. 'You know, I can't believe I just said that,' he said.

'Am I missing something there?' I asked Kelly now. As parties went, it was hardly the hot ticket of the century, but it was surprising – or rather, it wasn't at all surprising – how much mess could be made by a dozen over-excited pre-pubescents in a confined space. They'd done a respectable job of clearing up and Mrs Hinchcliffe had been like a human dynamo helping out, but there was something about that age group that defied logic. Everywhere I looked there seemed to be cake crumbs lurking behind desk and chair legs, bits of streamer (every year I said it: I *must* stop doing streamers) and various shreds and shards of brightly coloured foil, glinting accusingly wherever my glance came to rest. 'Jeez,' I said, climbing on a chair to retrieve a chocolate mini-roll wrapper that had somehow ended up stuck to the top edge of my map of the world. 'How did this make it to Alaska unnoticed?'

'There are forces at work here that defy human logic,' Kelly said sagely, as she made under-furniture forays with the 'bumper' broom – so named by the kids because it was too wide to be useful in a classroom situation, really, bumping into legs (animal and mineral) everywhere it went. 'Anyway, you were saying? What sort of something?'

'With Imogen and Henry,' I said. 'Mr Hinchcliffe was telling me earlier that he was going there for tea on Saturday and that he's been before. Seems an unlikely sort of pairing.'

'Oh, it's not, actually,' Kelly said. 'I was talking to his mum earlier on about it. It seems Imogen's grandparents only live a couple of streets away from where Henry does. She tells me they've taken to walking to school and back together.'

'Oh my God! Of course! That definitely all makes sense. It must have been Henry, then. Not Ben!'

'Henry what?'

'Henry who wrote "I fancy Imogen" on his secret note. Remember when I got them to do secrets in the hope of coaxing Imogen to share one? Well, that was one of them – and I just assumed it must be Ben. I mean, Henry? You'd never know it from they way they are in here, would you?'

Kelly grinned. 'You kidding? Can you imagine the stick Henry would get off the other boys?'

'Fair point, O wise one. Ah, but that's nice. Nice to know.'

'Nice for Henry, particularly,' Kelly agreed. 'I think Grandad's taken quite a shine to him. Did he tell you about the sledge?'

'Yes, he did. Bless him. That's so kind of him. You know, I got him all wrong when we first met, I think.'

'Oh, I don't think you did. I think he's just had a bit of an education himself. He reminds me of my grandad, actually. The sort of man who's never happier than when he's tucked away doing man-things – playing with tools and whittling wood, and smelling of Swarfega.'

I remembered the wood, then. The armful he'd brought home when I'd been round there a couple of weeks back. A proper man's man. The sort of man a boy like Henry could learn a lot from. Bless, I thought again. How very nice.

'You know what?' I said, plucking a length of streamer from a push-pin that was skewering Switzerland. 'I feel very Christmassy all of a sudden. Any mince pies left?'

'Pies?' Kelly snorted, shaking her head. 'Wrong p. There's only one p I'm interested in tonight. Same as Gary, and Jim, and Julia, and possibly even Don. P for *pub*.'

# Chapter 22

I knew I must have overslept when I opened my eyes and saw a slice of light shining whitely through the centre of the curtains and tracking its way across the floor and up onto the bed.

Either that or it had snowed in the night. Might it have? Now that would *really* be the icing on the cake. But there was none forecast – not yet anyway – even though there were some encouraging Met Office rumblings. And in the meantime there were things to do, people to see, places to go. Christmas wasn't going to organise itself, after all. And I had just three days left to 'elf' it into being.

I turned to check the time on my alarm clock, to find that it was already gone nine. Scandalously late for a lark like me, but, actually, who cared? Riley must have decided to let me lie in because I'd definitely not heard her. In full-on Riley-off-to-work mode she could wake the dead. Mind you, I'd gone to sleep late – I'd been awake well into the wee hours, reading. The book was still where I'd dropped it, in fact, forming a little tent on the bedroom floor. I reached down for it and placed it on my bedside table, smiling as I headed to the shower.

It had been a particularly emotional last day of term, the day before. I suppose it's always a little emotional when you reach the end of any term – not least because you tend to be at the end of your mental tether anyway, so the slightest little thing can set you off. And I was already a bit on the wet side when the day started anyway, Kieron having come home the previous evening with the announcement that he had asked a girl out on a date. Her name was Crystal and they were going to see some indie band called Brash, this coming weekend.

And as Mike observed, after Kieron had trotted upstairs to change, he'd looked almost as shocked by this development as we had, having spent all his teenage years up to that point pointing out that he 'didn't do girls'.

Plus there was the small matter of Riley, who had been officially recognised as David's girlfriend, when he had given her a pre-Christmas gift of a ring. No, *not* an engagement ring, she had been quick to point out, but just a symbol of how much she meant to him.

So there was no chance of me getting through the day without a tear in my eye even if you didn't factor in my little brood in school.

And I'd barely entered the premises before the ordeal began, because Shona was waiting for me just outside the reception doors when I arrived. I knew it was me she'd been waiting for because as soon as she saw me coming up the steps she peeled herself away from the wall and headed straight for me.

'Shall I help you with one of your bags, Miss?' she asked shyly when I drew level with her.

Being five foot nothing definitely had its advantages, I decided, as I thanked her and let her take some of the strain for me. One day I'd get streamlined or rationalised, or whatever it was, so that I didn't hoick quite so much to and fro every day. In the meantime, I was grateful for any help I could get, and Shona, though not a big girl, was definitely a growing one. She had sprouted at least a couple of inches in the short time she'd been with me.

'So, how are things going?' I asked her, as we walked the familiar route to my classroom.

'Okay, Miss,' she said. 'I'm enjoying being back in my class again a bit more now. I mean, I'm going to miss you and everyone in the Unit,' she added hurriedly. 'Specially Molly and Imogen, but it's nice to be back with all my friends.'

'And I'll bet they'll be glad to have you back,' I said. 'Our loss – and it is a loss, losing my super-brilliant organiser – is definitely their gain.'

I pulled my keys from my bag and got the classroom door open. There was still a faint whiff of party about the place. Difficult to define, probably even harder to analyse, but very much present all the same. 'And how are things at home now?' I asked Shona as she followed me in and put my satchel on my desk for me. 'How are *you* doing, sweetheart? You managing okay?'

'That's what I came to see you about,' she said, shrugging off her backpack and putting it on the desk in front of her. 'We're going away, Miss. To a place called Center Parcs. Have you heard of it?'

I nodded. 'Indeed I have,' I said. 'Wow, how exciting. For Christmas?'

'And New Year, too. We're going on Friday. My Auntie decided we'd have more fun there. You know … because there's lots to do there, and everything. There's a big indoor swimming pool and a huge play area for my cousins, and you can go bowling and I think they even have an ice rink. And you stay in a house in the forest, like a proper cabin. I saw pictures in the brochure. It looks really good.'

And so much better, I thought, than staying in a house steeped in recent pain, stuffed with bitter-sweet memories and shot through with thoughts of a future that had been taken away, and with oh, so many hours to be filled. 'That sounds brilliant,' I agreed. 'Just the thing. I am properly jealous. Any room for a stowaway in your swimming bag?'

She smiled. She'd undone her backpack and now plunged a hand into it.

'I got you a present,' she said shyly, producing a card and a gift, the latter wrapped in silver paper liberally covered in cartoon robins.

'Aww, love, that's so sweet of you,' I began, taking it from her, and trailing off as I knew I probably wouldn't make it to the end.

'It's to say thank you,' she said. 'And sorry, as well. Because it means I won't be able to come in and help you get the classroom displays organised after all, will I? I'm so sorry. I was looking forward to it too.'

She was blushing furiously by now, and my eyes had filled with tears, so between us we made quite a pair. 'Come here,' I said, scooping her into my arms for a hug. 'I tell you what. The display situation is like my ironing pile at home. You think you're up to date and then when your back has turned it always piles straight back up again. Let's make a plan for you to help me over February half-term, then. How about that idea? There'll be several boards that will need changing again by then, won't there? But you must still stop by as soon as we're back and tell me all about your Center Parcs trips, promise? And we're bound to have lots of leftover goodies to use up, so I'll have posh biscuits for visitors then, too. In the meantime,' I added, letting her go and indulging in a sniff, 'I think I need to find yet *another* tissue!'

Of course getting showered with cards and gifts is all part of the business of working with children; not for nothing do all those 'Best teacher' and 'Thank you, Miss' cards – not to mention mugs and teddies – mysteriously appear in all the shops come July. But it's not something you ever get cynical about, either. Yes, for sure, some come as the result of mums thinking 'Ah, that's a thought!' while pushing a trolley round ASDA – I'd done it myself, plenty of times.

And that was fine – they way I looked at it, such gifts and cards spoke volumes too. If a parent felt moved to get a present for a child to bring into school for their teacher, it seemed to me the child was probably not coming home from school every day telling their parents that 'Mr or Mrs so-and-so is a pig'. No, it probably meant, on balance, that things were going okay. That was the way I liked to think about it anyway.

Sometimes, however, presents couldn't help but make you cry, and that was an end to it. My heart card – in pride of place on the mantelpiece, as I'd promised – still choked me up every time I passed it, and if I'd thought I'd got away with it once Shona had hurried off to registration, then I was a fool – which I wasn't, so I didn't.

In the meantime, however, I needed to dry my eyes, stash Shona's present away ready to put under the tree once I was home, put the kettle on and get the first period organised. Because the last day of term was notorious not just for wellings up from wet women, it was also, tradition-ally, the day in the termly calendar where, for reasons that had never become completely clear to anyone, the kids had formed the impression that they didn't have to do any work.

'No,' I remember saying on the last day of the first term I had ever worked there, 'it's the last day of term, not the first day of the holidays. That's what happens tomorrow.' It had mostly got me nowhere.

Still it, could have been worse; the last day of the summer term (the end of the school year, of course) was so entrenched as a non-day that many of the older pupils, for a time, didn't even bother to show up. It was only when Mr Moore had had one of his periodic crack-downs that the truancy numbers for the day started to plummet. It was truly amazing, as he was fond of recounting, how many seemingly intelligent parents took their teenage children's protestations that the day was 'optional' at face value. And even among those who didn't, just how many were swayed by the seriously old chestnut of 'none of my friends' parents are making them go in'.

There was no danger of that happening in the Unit. Though Jim and Kelly and I had been clear that today was a school day, and should be treated as such, that didn't mean we hadn't planned plenty of fun activities.

And one of the constants in my little group – and this seemed to hold true, whatever the mixture of children at any one time – was that there was always a proportion for whom the business of sitting nicely was only marginally less difficult than it would be for an excitable six-year-old.

And, as if on cue, it was Gavin who was first into the classroom, doing his usual manoeuvre of sweeping in, as if propelled by an invisible cattle prod, then seeing me, remembering that speed wasn't *always* of the essence, and pulling up so quickly that if he'd been a character in a cartoon he would have had those little puffs of smoke drawn behind his feet.

'Miss!' he said, skidding to a halt. 'Miss! Guess what?'

I smiled at him and guided him to his seat, gently but firmly. 'Um, you've discovered the secrets of the universe?'

'No, Miss, don't be silly! You know I had that 'pointment with the doc? You know, in case I was mental? Well, I had to go back last night an' you'll never guess what.'

'What, Gavin?'

'He said I'm not North Polar! I'm a completely normal kid, is what he said. Can you believe it? An' my mum swore I was North Polar! But I'm not. Isn't that good? I just have my ADHD and that's it!'

245

I laughed out loud at that. Well, once I backtracked to what he'd put in his note for the secrets box about being referred, and as a consequence worked out what he was on about, anyway. Bless him. I couldn't help it.

'That's great news, Gav,' I agreed. 'Imagine that, eh? By the way, you know Santa lives at the North Pole, don't you?'

'Don't be daft, Miss, there's no such thing as Santa. *Everyone* knows that. Only reindeers. Oh, and polar bears. Lots of them.'

We didn't bother with lessons on the last day, not in the usual sense; I just liked to recap on what we'd learned over the term, looking back at some of our activities, the evidence of which was on the boards all around us – and which would be coming down at some point ready for next term. And a change of kids, in some cases, I thought as I watched them, and reflected on the friendships that had been made.

Good ones, I hoped, some of them – and that all-important camaraderie. Something I saw again and again as kids went up through school. Whatever they did, whatever classes they went through and where, once they'd forged a relationship with the Unit, with me and the team, and with each other, it was like an invisible bond they shared – one that didn't break.

Though it was limbs that I was slightly more concerned about breaking when Kelly and Gary Clark arrived to spend an hour with us, and that the latter had a game of Twister under his arm. Hardly the sort of thing you'd expect from our professional Child Protection Officer, much less a lesson, but then again, didn't it count as PE? Our new girl Gemma even got into the spirit of it all, and it was delightful to hear her shrieking with laughter as she tried to follow Imogen's instructions – and, as a consequence, inevitably landed flat on her face.

All in all, it was a great day and a very emotional one too. I hated goodbyes, even if I was going to see them all next term. 'You're such a wuss, Miss,' observed Henry, watching the tears slide down my cheeks as I tearfully hugged them all in turn before they left. Then it was my turn to go home and, despite my initial reservations, I finished the term in exactly the same frame of mind as I'd started it – tired but happy and with a sense of excited anticipation about what the new term might bring.

I also recalled Don's words about end-of-term-itis. And though I didn't feel quite burnt out, the twinkly lights of home were calling, and I knew I was ready to flick off my classroom light switch for the final time.

I picked the book up now, and placed it back on my bedside table before opening the curtains to let in a new day – the first day of two glorious weeks of Christmas holidays. It was a new copy of *Double Act*, the Jacqueline Wilson book Gavin had ripped the pages from, and I smiled at the note Imogen had written on the flyleaf about how reading about Garnet and Ruby and their dad's new girlfriend, Rosie, had made her realise she wasn't the only one who was sad. I flipped it over to the back cover and read the start of the blurb: *No one can ever be like a mother to us, especially not stupid frizzy dizzy Rose!* It made me wonder again why I had forgotten the true significance of this book, of why it had seemed so important to Imogen.

She must have delivered her secret gift by stealth the previous afternoon, because I'd not left the classroom, but I had no memory of anyone going over and putting it on my desk. But there it was anyway, neatly wrapped and tied with curling ribbon, and, judging by the size and feel when I picked it up, a book.

I'd looked at the tag attached to it, and I'd smiled. It was hand-made, with deckled edges, and it took me straight to a memory – a much-cherished memory from my own childhood. A memory of when my sister and I would sit down at the dining table with our mum and start officially 'doing' Christmas. We'd do it every year, and it would almost always be a cold, wintery evening – making garlands out of strips of coloured paper she'd have bought in Woolworths, creating snowflakes out of circles of tissue, carefully folded and snipped, and making gift tags from the previous year's cards. It was quite a privilege, as it involved using my mum's big metal pinking shears, which, being meant for sewing and easily blunted, were usually out of bounds.

A legacy of the post-war years – or the make-do-and-mend years, as my mum always called them – it was the sort of thing you didn't see much any more. I flipped the tag over, and there, just as I'd suspected, was Imogen's small, careful handwriting. '*Dear Miss*,' she'd written, '*Merry Christmas!*' Then there were brackets, between which she'd underlined a second message, namely '*Pleeease don't open this till you get home!*'

248

And I'd missed her, the minx, but I didn't blame her. No matter how far she'd come or how relaxed she now seemed, she was still, I felt, a quiet girl at heart. Never an attention-seeker, I knew she would have probably found it daunting to have actually given whatever this was to me herself.

And that was fine. I'd duly popped it in my bag before finally heading home, and, though my first plan had been to put it under the tree with all the other presents, it had called to me, somehow, as the evening had gone on, because I think, on some level, I already knew what was inside. And I'd read it, cover to cover, learned all about Ruby and Garnet, who'd also lost a mum and gained a step-mum, and it made me think and, mostly, made me cry.

'This is definitely the way to do it,' Riley observed as we pushed a laden trolley round our giant out-of-town super-market. It was eleventh-hour shopping and it was eight in the evening; not my usual way of doing things at all. But when your daughter offers to come and help you do all the shopping once she's home from work, you don't refuse. Well, I don't. I'm not that mad.

'You see, Mum?' she continued. 'That's where people always get it wrong, isn't it? They all rush around like luna-tics trying to get everything done early, which means they're all fighting each other over the tins of Quality Street and arguing over spaces in the car park, whereas, actually, if you just hold your nerve in these situations, look' – she cast an expansive arm around her – 'isn't this so much better? This place is almost empty!'

I smiled as I weighed up the merits of a BOGOF on nuts. Wouldn't I just end up throwing half of them away in March? Oh, to be 18 again, I thought. To be at a place in your life when 'Will they run out of turkeys?' is not a question that ever enters your head. Or to be like Mike, perhaps, whose Christmas 'preparations' these days consisted of a) getting the decorations out of the loft for me, and b) going into town to buy half a dozen presents at teatime on Christmas Eve. Oh, if only.

'You're right about that,' I said, taking the box of cereal that Riley had got down from a high shelf from me. How did my daughter get to be five foot quite something when I was five foot absolutely nothing? 'But, as you might have already noticed, the veg aisle is half empty as well.'

Riley grinned. 'Mother, trust me, the world won't go to hell in a handcart for want of a few minging sprouts on our plates. In fact, it'll be a much nicer place, when you think about it, won't it?' She laughed then, wrinkling her nose. 'And on *so* many levels.'

And, of course, she was right, and I was just about to agree with her when we rounded the aisle to find ourselves trolley nose to trolley nose with two familiar faces – those of Imogen and her grandfather.

'Well, I never!' I said. 'Fancy seeing you here!'

Though, actually, it wasn't such a big shock to do so because though I'd never seen Imogen there – she hadn't lived round our way before, had she? – bumping into pupils and former pupils was a common occurrence. Pretty much all of the local teenagers attended the school I worked at, so it would have been surprising *not* to bump into them.

But to bump into this one at this time was particularly pleasing, because it meant I could thank her for her present in person.

So I did, adding that I had read the whole book from cover to cover, the previous night. 'In bed, like I used to do when I was your age,' I confided. 'Because once I started it I just couldn't put it down.'

'I'm glad you liked it,' she said shyly.

'I *loved* it,' I corrected. 'And I can also see why it's meant so much to you,' I added, meeting her gaze and lightly touching her forearm. I could see she was squirming slightly, and I absolutely understood, so I didn't want to make too big a thing of it. 'Anyway, what brings you here?' I added. 'Oh, this is my daughter Riley, by the way. As you can see, we're trying to get Christmas organised, *finally*. Though I'm sure there are better things to be doing than wheeling a trolley round a supermarket right now, eh?'

'Last-minute list,' Mr Hinchcliffe said, waving a small piece of paper. 'We've been dispatched, haven't we, Immie? Nan's orders.'

'And to get some bedding for me, as well,' Imogen added excitedly. 'Daddy sent some money so I can choose a new duvet cover and curtains. He's decorating my bedroom ready for when I go back after Christmas.'

'How lovely,' I said, peering into their trolley, 'and let me see … is it, by any chance, going to be pink?'

'Bright pink,' Imogen said, grinning. 'But not with princesses or anything. I didn't want princesses or fairies or any of that girly-girly stuff. It's going to be pink and purple butterflies. Daddy's even painting some on the wall. But

251

I'm still staying at Nan and Grandad's sometimes, aren't I, Grandad?' she added, with a touching sensibility. 'I'm still going to live there when Daddy's away working.' She grinned up at him. 'So now I'll have two bedrooms!'

'Ooh, I am *so* jealous,' Riley said, with feeling. 'I would *love* to have two bedrooms. All that space!'

'That's because you need two just to create a bit of floor-space,' I pointed out. 'She is very, *very* messy,' I stage-whispered to Imogen, from behind my hand. 'And speaking of mess – well, in a manner of speaking – how is project sledge coming on? All built and ready to roll yet?'

Mr Hinchcliffe nodded. 'It is. Well, very nearly. Just another coat of varnish and it'll be ready for action. Just need a bit of snow now, and the two of them can take it out for a proper road-test.'

I smiled at Imogen. 'So Henry did a pretty good job, then?'

'He did indeed,' said Mr Hinchcliffe. 'Young Henry's quite a dab hand with a saw, isn't he, Immie?'

But the girl herself had fallen silent. She was too busy blushing. She had gone as pink as the butterflies her dad was painting in her bedroom – as pink as the tips of her pretty hair. Mr Hinchcliffe and Riley and I all exchanged grins. So it seemed Imogen and Henry had really struck up quite a friendship. And was that so surprising? They would both soon be 14, after all.

'What's the matter, Im?' her grandad teased. 'Has the cat got your tongue, love?'

And the smile on Imogen's face was a thing of such beauty. Riley was right. You really didn't need sprouts to make your Christmas. You didn't really need a turkey, come to that. It was cheesy – seriously-make-your-toes-curl-cheesy – but it was also true. Sometimes – in fact most times, if you were talking about life's priorities – a smile on a child's face would do.

# Epilogue

Once Gerri was out of the picture, and things settled down for her at home, Imogen came on in the proverbial leaps and bounds. She returned to the Unit after Christmas but wasn't far behind Shona and Gavin in settling back into a mainstream class, where her speech and her confidence gradually returned to her.

As anticipated, Imogen was able to move back into her dad's house early in the New Year, but would always return to stay with her grandparents on days when her dad was on trips abroad. She also continued to have a good friend in Henry, who became something of a regular round at her grandparents for a time, and – for a time, anyway, a little further down the line – in her love life.

In the longer term, Imogen's father and Gerri divorced, though not before her trial for abuse and wilful neglect came to court. She was lucky – because her solicitor painted such a grim picture of her own childhood, she was given a suspended sentence and was ordered to attend counselling.

She was also ordered not to contact Imogen and her father ever again.

As for the rest of my little brood, they all trundled on through their teens and, as was to be expected, because that's the way of things, some thrived and blossomed, while some continued to wrestle with their challenges. Shona went on to do very well academically, and became quite a regular when I needed help with my displays, and little Molly definitely reached her potential. Gavin too, though still medicated all the way through his schooling, turned out to be quite the academic, and the older he became, the less obvious were his symptoms. And though poor Ben never really got any less challenging, he managed to endure long periods in school with relatively few exclusions for fighting. His father was also allocated a family support worker to help him better support Ben at home.

And, as for me, well, I was just hitting my stride with little Imogen. New Year, new challenges, new problems to be tackled. I couldn't wait to meet my next batch of pupils when I came back that following January, because for everything I helped them with I knew they'd teach me so much too. And needless to say, they didn't let me down …

Childline: 0800 1111
www.childline.org.uk

# CASEY WATSON

One woman determined to make a difference.

Read Casey's poignant memoirs and be inspired.

Five-year-old Justin was desperate and helpless

Six years after being taken into care, Justin has had 20 failed placements. Casey and her family are his last hope.

**THE BOY NO ONE LOVED**

A damaged girl haunted by her past

Sophia pushes Casey to the limits, threatening the safety of the whole family. Can Casey make a difference in time?

**CRYING FOR HELP**

Abused siblings who do not know what it means to be loved

With new-found security and trust, Casey helps Ashton and Olivia to rebuild their lives.

## LITTLE PRISONERS

Branded 'vicious and evil', 8-year-old Spencer asks to be taken into care

Casey and her family are disgusted: kids aren't born evil. Despite the challenges Spencer brings, they are determined to help him find a loving home.

## TOO HURT TO STAY

A young girl secretly caring for her mother

Abigail has been dealing with pressures no child should face. Casey has the difficult challenge of helping her to learn to let go.

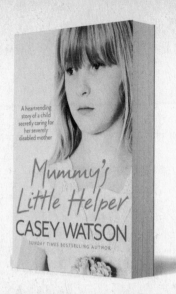

MUMMY'S LITTLE HELPER

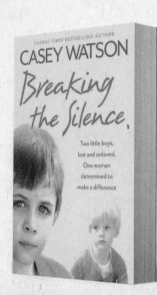

Two boys with an unlikely bond

With Georgie and Jenson Casey is facing her toughest test yet.

BREAKING THE SILENCE

# FEEL HEART.
# FEEL HOPE.
# READ CASEY.

Discover more about Casey Watson.
Visit www.caseywatson.co.uk

Find Casey Watson on  &

# Moving Memoirs

Stories of hope, courage and the power of love…

If you loved this book, then you will love our
Moving Memoirs eNewsletter

## Sign up to…

- Be the first to hear about new books

- Get sneak previews from your favourite authors

- Read exclusive interviews

- Be entered into our monthly prize draw to win one
  of our latest releases before it's even hit the shops!

## Sign up at

**www.moving-memoirs.com**